The Ascent of the New World Order:

Birth of a world government.

By

Christopher J. Russell

Acknowledgements

*My thanks go to Linda Jane and Barbara
for their continuous support and encouragement.*

Our world has seen much of the human condition through-out recorded history. Yet this human condition addresses a lot more than just birth, growth, emotionality, aspiration, conflict, and mortality. As the planet has progressed on its enigmatic journey through the cosmos, it has seen human beings degenerate from using their intelligence to survive and flourish upon the land, to attempting, successfully on many occasions, to control and change nature, bending it to suit their own desires.

Where once people would live for the large part peaceable lives, giving Mother Nature the respect she deserves, trying to use natural resources as wisely as possible and avoiding damaging the eco-system to a point where it can no longer recover, we all, as a species, have aided in the pointless destruction of all that is there to keep us alive.

Where once spirituality had some true meaning, in the modern age this appears no longer to be the case. Very few human beings seem to be in tune with nature and the universe around them, in the modern world spirituality is dominated by religions that desire power and wealth, causing much in the way of damage as they force their way around the world. Piety oozes from the followers of western religions like some toxic chemical, causing distress and devastation wherever it goes and upon whosoever it touches. All the while these religions make great use of propaganda, demonstrating the good deeds that they have done, aiding the less fortunate, giving food and medical assistance to those who need it. The naïve among the populations marvel at such acts of kindness and offer donations. Yet in many cases it is the very religions themselves that have had some fundamental connection in the creation of whatever catastrophe has befallen the unfortunate souls that are in need of help.

Those within the higher echelons of these religions continuously affect the lives of their followers, advising them of the rights and wrongs of any given social matter, all the while flouting the very book that they profess to follow. These religions are incredibly wealthy, the elite within which wield immense power and influence. All too often these religious bodies fall easily under the influence of a global elite that manipulates populations for their own gain. If one wanted proof of these points one should look at the financial investments of the major religions, they are not insignificant, they stretch out with an almost rhyzomic effect. While the elite of any religion live in comparative luxury, beautiful homes, fine clothing and good food, there are people suffering and dying but for a few scraps of food and a little medical care.

*****

The world within which we live changed considerably throughout the twentieth century and has continued to change drastically into the twenty-first century. Wars, political change and corruption, climate change, false flag operations and much, much more have all taken their effect on the world and the people who live in it. To a large extent these effects have not had a positive outcome for the majority of people, in fact quite the opposite, a very small minority of individuals have profited at the expense of everyone else.

As we are all aware, we now live in a world dominated by technology. In itself, technology is neither good nor bad, it is neutral in its basic form. The uses to which technology is put dictates whether it is good or bad. Simple examples of just two different uses are:

1. Medically based technology such as Medical Resonance Imaging (MRI), (Figure. 1). A procedure that many people will have come across and may well have been instrumental in saving their lives through the discovery of a number of conditions. This is obviously an example where technology has been put to a very good and positive use.

6

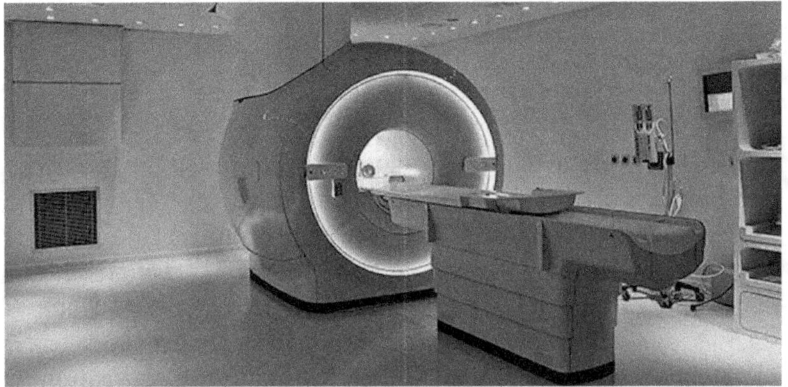

Fig.1

CoreB-MRI, (Medical Resonance Imaging).

2. Military based technology such as nuclear weaponry, nuclear submarines (Figure. 2) or weapons that are developed from this type of technology. An example of this type of technological usage would be artillery shells that contain depleted Uranium. This is obviously an example where technology has been put to a very bad, negative and lethal use.

Fig.2

Ohio-class submarine USS Rhode Island (SSBN 740)

It is interesting to note that proportionally, more of a country's financial expenditure is spent on weaponry, such as nuclear weapons, than is spent on medical and social needs of the population.

There are other types of technology that can fall within either of the positive or negative categories. The view taken by the individual within a society with regard to the particular uses of this type of technology will dictate whether it is in fact positive or negative. This subjectivity is dependent on numerous factors such as; social awareness, knowledge of the subject matter and social capital networking – which would include, economic, educational and personal networks.

Nuclear power stations are one of the technologies that can fall into either category dependent on the opinion of the individual. This source of energy provides much of the power that society presently requires, therefore it is the positive side of this type of technology. Yet, on the opposite side of the coin, this type of power production does not, as is popularly portrayed, supply energy without waste and this waste cannot be disposed of safely. It may as society is told, be relatively safe for the present population, but for their children and grandchildren the threat of contamination will be a real and constant threat.

Another point with regard to Nuclear power stations worth mentioning is that of damage either accidental or through 'act of God', to these power stations.

On the 26 April, 1986, the Chernobyl nuclear power station in the Ukraine, then still a part of the Russian block, suffered a catastrophic accident. There were numerous deaths and the entire area around the power station was severely and negatively affected. The effects of radiation have and will affect the population for many years to come through such things as radiation-induced cancer and leukaemia. This may seem to many to be something that only happens in the past, or perhaps something that occurs rarely enough to be worth 'taking the risk', but it is doubtful that this view would be held by those who suffered and will suffer horrendously, due to the elites of this world misleading populations as to the worth of this type of power production. The Chernobyl incident is not a 'one off' occurrence.

On March 28, 1979, the Three Mile Island nuclear power station, in Dauphin County, Pennsylvania, United States, suffered a failure that allowed the release of radioactive material into the surrounding area.   Controversy concerning the effects of the radiation released is still ongoing. Epidemiology studies stating that there were no recognizable long term health effects conflicted with anecdotal local evidence. The fact that according to the World Nuclear Association, the clean-up took twelve years and cost approximately 973 million dollars, should raise concern as to the validity of the findings of these studies.

In March of 2011, the nuclear power station at Fukushima in Japan suffered a catastrophic meltdown due to an earthquake and a tsunami that followed shortly afterwards.

According to the Greenpeace website, the environment has suffered considerably through higher levels of radiation affecting both the fauna and flora, and has also affected the lives of almost one hundred thousand people, many of whom will not be able to return to their homes. Yet the government is informing the local population and the world in general that the situation is returning back to normal. Again, according to Greenpeace this just is not the case, if people were to return to their homes, then in many cases they would be living where radiation levels are too high and would still be surrounded by contamination.

It should be noted that not all official or officially funded reports or studies can be taken as either factual or truthful. It is the social, political and industrial elites of the world that inform the population of what the 'truth' is, what is morally and ethically acceptable. In this way a powerful elite gain control of an individual's beliefs and values. The elite elements of the world do without question follow their own agenda, immaterial of the impact and devastation that their words and decisions can and do have on the population as a whole.

One method presently used by the elite of any country to enable and improve control over a given population is through the continuous monitoring of that population. In the modern age one simple method of monitoring any population is through the use of closed circuit television cameras or CCTV.

The United Kingdom has more closed circuit television (CCTV), (Figure. 3) than any other country in the world. This knowledge will make many people in the UK feel mentally reassured and safer in their everyday lives. This is because the state tells them that they are safer. The same statement can be made for every other country that has CCTV coverage. But this is not necessarily the case. Let us address a few simple points:

1.) With such extensive CCTV coverage there is, as the system tells us, less crime. Well, if one adheres to the governmentally produced figures, then this would seem to be the case. We are told that crime figures show that levels of certain types of crimes have fallen considerably since the introduction of CCTV. We live in a safer country.

Fig.3

Surveillance, CCTV in the United Kingdom.

http://www.cctvforum.com/

This is not necessarily the case. Empirical evidence, just looking about the area, city, town, village that you live in will show differently. Each day the news programmes on the television, the daily papers and the internet all report a multitude of crimes. Each and every day crimes are still committed. These crimes include, Murder, Rape, people being Attacked and/or mugged and robberies taking place to mention but a few. Peculiarly enough, the same crimes as before CCTV was installed.

2. Due to the levels of CCTV through a country, more criminals are caught for the crimes that they commit and are removed from society.

Again, this is not necessarily the case. As can be seen from the general media, just as many crimes go unsolved as before the introduction of CCTV. People are still murdered, raped, have acts of violence committed against them and the perpetrator's identities remain unknown.

3. The threat of terrorism gives just cause for the extreme levels of CCTV in the UK. Without the CCTV coverage that exists in the UK there would be many more terrorist attacks and therefore many more people killed or injured as a result of these supposed attacks. This means that CCTV has become an essential component in deterring any would be terrorists, or that terrorists are easily caught whilst planning, carrying out or having committed these horrendous acts.

Yet once more reality and governmental assessment do not coincide. It is reasonable to assume that if terrorists are determined to execute such horrific acts, then the planning would be undertaken out of sight of any CCTV. From the point of view of a terrorist, it would be advantageous for the actual act of committing a bombing or some other equally heinous act to be recorded on CCTV. The CCTV footage and or images of the aforesaid would at some time be played on news programmes and other social media, thus furthering the desired results of the terrorist's actions, that of creating fear, panic and alarm. So if anything, CCTV could be relied upon by terrorists to support their fundamental aim.

The idea of 'terrorism' has been used many times to ensure that the population acquiesce to the wishes of authoritative bodies. Making the public believe that foreign activists and insurgents are 'around every corner', waiting to pounce at the earliest opportunity, creates an atmosphere of underlying fear that permeates through-out society. The insertion of CCTV into towns and cities is one method by which both the population are mistakenly pacified, and the elite are able to ensure constant surveillance of the masses with supposed justification.

The words of James Madison, the fourth President of the United States have greater meaning in the modern age than any other,

"If Tyranny and Oppression come to this land, it will be in the guise of fighting a foreign enemy."

(https://www.brainyquote.com/quotes/authors/j/james_madison.html)

A thought-provoking point with regard to CCTV is that of the supposed failure of the CCTV systems at critical moments. There are two initial points that come to mind:

1. On the occasion when Princess Diana died, the car she was in hit a concrete post in Paris in the Pont de l'Alma tunnel (Figure. 4). The CCTV in the tunnel was not working. It is sad that at such a vital moment in history, the very items that could have both shown what actually happened and allowed improvements to be made to the road system, were not functioning.

Fig.4

Pont de l'Alma tunnel, Paris.

2. In London on the 7th of July 2005, the CCTV on the Tavistock Square bus on which a suicide bomber killed both himself and sadly, killed and injured a number of other people was also not working.

The monitoring of any population through such means as CCTV undermines the very notion of a true democracy. That the population should be monitored utilising outside threats such as terrorism, should raise concerned voices within even the most conservative elements of society.

The United Kingdom has, contradicting popular belief, never been a true democracy. The way in which the governmental bodies do and always have functioned, added to the fact that the head of state is royalty, the Queen, proves this to be an indisputable fact. With this said, it should be noted that as of the year 2016 the United Kingdom government has finally left all pretence of democracy behind. In 2016 the government of the United Kingdom brought into law the ability for G.C.H.Q, (Government Communications Head Quarters), (Figure. 5), to legally monitor all communications. This includes; all telecommunications, any and all internet traffic including e-mails and texts. The pretext for this unprecedented action is that of

National Security, the need to safeguard the general population from actual or possible terrorist attacks.

The reality of the situation is somewhat different as will be seen. Although there is little doubt that terrorists could possibly use the internet to carry out their own nefarious plans to a limited degree, it is highly doubtful that they can go any further than this,

Fig.5

Government Communications Head Quarters, (G.C.H.Q).
(The Doughnut).

https://www.gchq.gov.uk/news

unless of course terrorists have magically gained the scientific ability to be able to send explosive devices along either telephone cables or via wireless connections. The only justification that exists for which any communications associated with the general population should be monitored, is if there is already solid foundation for the belief that certain individuals are undertaking or planning to undertake illegal actions that will or could cause harm to members of the general population. Even in this situation, the monitoring of communications should only be undertaken with the agreement of a court of law and only after sufficient proof has been produced. This, as of 2016 is no longer the case; representation to a British court of law by the Security Services has been bypassed.

What should be noted is that for all the faith in and use of technology, the role that the police force and the security services play in catching and or stopping crimes is not insubstantial. The same should be said of terrorist attacks that are thwarted. Technology may well play a part in stopping or curtailing the actions that are attempted by these terrorists, but it is the security services and the police forces within the UK that have the job of being on the front line. The work that they do cannot and should not be underestimated. They are both the first and last line of defence for the society within which we live. One must remember that it is those individuals who 'Put their lives on the line', not the decision makers in their lofty and comfortable offices in Whitehall. The egotistical sycophants of Whitehall, the politicians and high level civil servants who arbitrarily make decisions affecting the population of this country, do not go and with the exception of but a few, have not ever been 'on the ground'. The opposite as stated earlier with regard of the police force is the case. The vast majority of police officers in the UK do actually care about our society and those of us within it. They do try to make a difference and improve the lives of those around them, and as such they should be commended for their tenacity and perseverance.

The job that they have is in many regards a thankless one. They walk a perilous line between the demands of the Whitehall bureaucrats and politicians which they are obliged to enforce, while at the same time attempting to keep the general population safe. This is often an almost impossible task. When one realises that those in Whitehall, not all, but certainly the majority, are purely following their own agenda such as their careers prospects, then one can see how difficult the job of those in the police force has actually become. Idiotic and or unproductive laws passed often infuriate the public whose resentments are taken out upon those 'on the ground', those in the police force.

Affluence and Control

Technology does have many different facets in the modern world and if used correctly could be of great advantage to all who live on this planet. It is quite apparent from the number of people suffering in so many horrible ways that technology or the lack of technology, is being used by what one can only call the 'elite' of society for their personal advancement both politically and financially, encroaching on the lives and freedoms of everyone else. There are people living around the world who, but for a very small amount of money, would have clean fresh water through the construction of water pumps. There are numerous diseases and illnesses running rife around the world, even in this so-called modern age of the 21st century. Many of these diseases and illnesses could be easily remedied. Science has created medicines and treatments that could be provided to assist the poor souls who are suffering, but as is normally the case, due to political and or financial factors, men, women and children suffer and die needlessly.

The amount of money in this world is staggering. Countries have national debts of trillions of dollars. The amounts are so large that it is difficult to envisage such enormous figures. One might think that many of these national debts have been accrued through social innovation and improvements for the populations, but that would be incorrect. If one were to address the national debt of the United States of America, it could be seen that the vast majority of the debt accumulated has not been amassed by the general population. The government decides where any monies go and therefore the government is responsible for the colossal debt. Yet, as simple as things may seem, it is far more complicated.

The United States government does not create its own money as one might have been led to believe. Instead, in 1913 the Federal Reserve was created which deals with the finances of the United States of America. One should bear in mind that the Federal Reserve is neither owned nor run by the American government, it is in effect a private company. This is most peculiar indeed when one realises that the United States does not actually create nor print its own money. The American government will turn to the Federal Reserve when it needs funds. The Federal Reserve creates the required funds from what can be described as the 'ether', it produces money from thin air, from nothing. This sounds ludicrous to anyone who might believe themselves to be a well-balanced individual, but it is the truth nonetheless. But it gets better as we move on. Once the Federal Reserve has manufactured and brought into existence this previously non-existent amount of money requested by the American government and delivered it as required, it then charges the American government and by logical extension the American people colossal levels of interest. To the average person in the street all this most probably means very little, if anything at all. Well, not only should it mean something to the average person in the street, but they should be rather concerned to put it mildly.

There was at one time something known as the Gold Standard. To put it crudely, the Gold Standard meant that the Dollar or any other currency that used the Gold Standard had real worth. You could theoretically take your paper money or promissory note (as that is all that paper money actually is), to a bank or other designated institution and have it exchanged for gold. Now, under President Nixon in the early 1970's, the Gold reserve was finally 'done away with' and 'Fiat' money took its place. All this might seem a little boring, until one realises that 'Fiat' money, the term 'Fiat' coming from the Latin, "let it become", "it will become", is currency established as money by governmental decree, a government says that the currency is real and useable by law. All very good so far. Yet, if you take your "Fiat" money, perhaps a twenty dollar bill or a ten pound note into a bank or other designated institution and request its true worth, the teller will respond by simply giving you smaller denominations of the same total amount that you gave across the counter. You would not be issued with twenty dollars or ten pounds worth of the precious metal, Gold. So what does it matter? You still have your twenty dollars or ten pounds. Yes, you do still have your money but, and this is the important point, without the Gold Standard to back the money, it has become worthless. It is intrinsically valueless money, used as money because of a government law, because a government says so.   When one considers the situation, it is rather amusing. So you are paying for goods that you need or want, and being paid for the services that you offer with nothing but bits of paper. Perhaps a better quality, but the same stuff that you can purchase from the local stationary store or shopping outlet. One might ask, "What difference does it make? We still get what we want. We still buy and eat what we want, we still have our homes, our cars, our clothes. So who cares?"

Well, they are very good points, we all still have all these things that we feel that we need for our lives to run smoothly. Yet, while the population through the government is borrowing money from the Federal Reserve and paying interest on something that does not and did not exist in the first place, the very prices that are being paid for the goods are continuously increasing. This increase (inflation) is not as is popularly portrayed, due to lack of resources, or any other such nonsense. It is purely and simply due in essence to the fact that the government needs to pay the Federal Reserve back the massive loans they have taken out. This is funded in the simplest of terms, by the population paying higher taxes. So, when a manufacturer is charged higher taxes to produce and sell their products, the cost is passed through the entire social chain.
As can be seen in Figure 6, the fluctuation in prices varied little prior to the foundation of the Federal Reserve.

This means that the consumer is paying extortionately more for their shopping, education, medical bills, fuel, etc. Now, if a government were to produce its own money, preferably and sensibly backed by something such as the Gold Standard, then the ridiculous and unnecessary rises in costs and therefore of inflation need not necessarily happen.

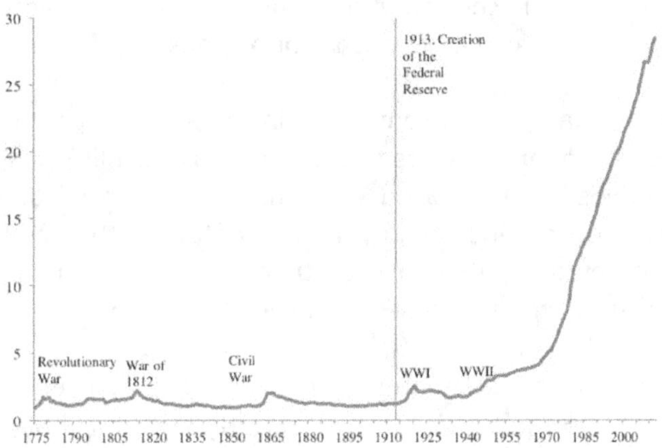

Sources: Bureau of Labor Statistics, Historical Statistics of the United States, and Reinhart and Rogoff (2009).

Fig.6

Business Insider, Markets

This having been said, governments are not as many people might think, solely responsible for the state of financial distress within both their own country and the world as a whole. The mistaken belief that governments are exclusively accountable is propagated by a social elite that controls the majority of the population of a given country and populations through-out the world. This elite element of society manipulates much of the population through numerous means and measures such as, food and water, energy and fuel and most notably, financially. If any government or prominent and popular leader of the people threatens the power base of the elite, either openly or inadvertently, perhaps by opting to leave the petro-dollar, or financially undermining the elite's power base through social improvements, then pressures are brought to bear. The means used more often than not will involve either elimination of the particular leader or war. In recent history the method used has been to create extreme civil unrest and often civil war. This has the effect of eradicating the initial obstruction and at the same time preparing the country/population for easy exploitation and manipulation at a later date.

There are many in society who will not only refuse to accept this observation, but will mock such propositions.

It is worth noting that prominence in the world of politics is not a prerequisite for influence to be exerted by the elite. One could be a pioneer in the world of technology, a social activist, a whistle-blower or include any number of factors that might have or be having a negative effect either now or in the near future with regard to the strategies of the elite.

The words often attributed, correctly or otherwise to Henry Kissinger, give much in the way of credibility to the above,

"Who controls the food supply controls the people; who controls the energy can control whole continents; who controls the money can control the world."

(Attributed to) Henry Kissinger, 1973

Although the veracity of the above attribution cannot be verified, that does not diminish the truth of the words.

It is generally assumed that money is the product result of the barter system, a necessary development in the advancement of human society. Although as human beings managed to function extremely well for hundreds of thousands of years without the existence of money, this line of thought is drawn into question. Money is neither a likely nor logical consequence of evolution, it is purely and simply a man-made creation generated and used as a mechanism of social control.

J.F.K

One man who was supposedly aiming at making a difference to the production, maintenance and control of finances within the twentieth century was President J. F. Kennedy. If this were the case, then he obviously saw what was happening with regard to the Federal Reserve and recognized that something needed to be done to remove the source of power from the wrong hands.
It has been said that one of his aims whilst in office, was to put an end to the production of money being in the hands of those who ran the Federal Reserve. Instead, the American government would be the sole producer of money for the American people. This would obviously be undertaken through initially small steps, the first of which was supposedly J.F.K's executive order 11110, the validity of this is still a strong point of contention. The effect would have been to stop what was and is in effect a private company from profiting at the expense of the American people. Thus also limiting the power that a private company, and therefore those in control of that company could have over the entire population.

It would seem that the vast majority of people are oblivious to the power that the Federal Reserve welds over and within their lives and the lives and laws of other nations. It is possible that President Kennedy had put the wheels in motion with respect to achieving the above, but due to his untimely death any motions that he had put in place to have this ratified in law were reversed by the incoming president, his replacement, Vice President, Lyndon B. Johnson.

So the Federal Reserve still retains colossal authoritative power both within the United States of America, and due to the influence that it has either directly or indirectly through financial organizations, over the rest of the world. One might be tempted to associate the death of President J. F. Kennedy directly with his decision to stop the Federal Reserve in its tracks, but this might not necessarily be the case. It is entirely possible and perhaps likely that his actions did enrage the oligarchs of the Federal

Reserve to the point where it would have appeared a good idea to remove him from power. But a man such as President J. F. Kennedy, a man legally elected by the people of America could only, realistically, be removed by impeachment, something that the American people would undoubtedly have rejected. To the Federal Reserve, Kennedy was indeed a very dangerous obstacle, but perhaps at this point it should be remembered that there were two other major undertakings that President Kennedy (Figure 7) was supposedly going to authorize.

Fig.7   President John F. Kennedy.

One of the undertakings would have been the breaking up of the CIA. The attempt by President J. F. Kennedy to break up the C.I.A would have been based on the need to restrict the power and influence that the organization wielded worldwide. The breaking up and/or dismantling of the CIA would not have threatened the security of the United States, but quite the opposite. If the sphere of influence of the CIA were controlled and regulated then disreputable governmental bodies and oligarchs within the United States would not have been able to use the organization for their own nefarious and perverse requirements around the world and at home. (It should be mentioned that the CIA does not or did not have mandate to operate within the confines of the Unites States homeland.) The result of reining in and limiting the CIA would have had a colossal effect on attitudes worldwide concerning the American nation. Without the United States wantonly tramping its way throughout the world, killing people and manipulating and or bringing about regime change with impunity, using the excuse of self-defence against possible threats, there may not have been total peace throughout the world, but there would without doubt have been fewer wars. Men, women and children of so many nations would not have suffered both horrendously and needlessly for the benefit of a limited number of Americans at the top, the elite and America would not be one of the most hated countries in the world.

A third point that President Kennedy was supposedly going to address was that of withdrawing American troops from Vietnam. The partaking in a conflict, such as America involving itself in the internal conflict between the North and South Vietnamese is to put it mildly irresponsible, highly questionable, arrogant and dependent on interpretation of international law, illegal. The outcome of the conflict was that thousands of very brave American servicemen gave their lives or were injured in a conflict for which American intervention should never have been sanctioned in the first place. Hundreds of thousands of Vietnamese people also suffered through loss of their families, appalling injuries from such disgusting weapons as Napalm and Agent Orange and/or death.

Had President Kennedy not been killed, then the dreadful loss of life and terrible injuries sustained by both sides in a conflict that need not have happened, would have been avoided.

When one addresses the three points together; firstly, the removing of power from the Federal Reserve, secondly, the breaking up of the CIA, and thirdly, the withdrawal of military forces from Vietnam; one can clearly see the huge and limiting effects that would have taken their toll on the controlling influence of those individuals within the military industrial complex. Through the aforementioned, it would be difficult for anyone, save for perhaps a naïve fool, to not notice solid motives for the removal of President J. F. Kennedy from his governmental office, via a bullet or two.

President Kennedy undoubtedly by his choice of future actions recognized that the American people were being lied to, used, and treated as cannon fodder for an elite element within society. At this point perhaps the words of President Eisenhower (Figure 8.) in his farewell address from the Whitehouse, January 17th 1961, to the American people would have a greater meaning to many:

"...we must guard against the acquisition of unwarranted influence, whether sort or unsort by the military industrial complex..."

President Eisenhower, January 17th 1961.

Fig.8   President Eisenhower, farewell speech.

President Eisenhower, January 17th 1961 - Bill Allen/AP

There is perhaps one other point that might have contributed to the untimely demise of President J. F. Kennedy.   In a speech at the Waldorf-Astoria Hotel on April 27, 1961, he referenced the need for the removal of secrecy from American society and society as a whole, he Stated,

"The very word "secrecy" is repugnant in a free and open society; and we are as a people inherently and historically opposed to secret societies, to secret oaths and secret proceedings. We decided long ago that the dangers of excessive and unwarranted concealment of pertinent facts far outweighed the dangers which are cited to justify it.
Even today, there is little value in opposing the threat of a closed society by imitating its arbitrary restrictions. Even today, there is little value in insuring the survival of our nation if our traditions do not survive with it. And there is very grave danger that an announced need for increased security will be seized upon those anxious to expand its meaning to the very limits of official censorship and concealment.
That I do not intend to permit to the extent that it is in my control. And no official of my Administration, whether his rank is high or low, civilian or military, should interpret my words here tonight as an excuse to censor the news, to stifle dissent, to cover up our mistakes or to withhold from the press and the public the facts they deserve to know.".

JOHN F. KENNEDY PRESIDENTIAL LIBRARY AND MUSEUM

This speech would without doubt and in conjunction with previous mentioned actions, have more than just concerned those of the military/industrial complex that President Eisenhower made reference to earlier in the year. That the President would definitely and defiantly be making enormous social, political, military and industrial changes would have had serious repercussions through-out the world   Power within American society and numerous countries around the world would once again reside to a larger extent with the people. The influence of the military industrial complex would have been severely undermined. With fewer wars, less people suffering and greater autonomy for poorer countries, there would have been improved options for such to pursue their own internal interests and improve their own societies. For the American people the freedoms that they had known and taken for granted for so long would no longer be in jeopardy of disappearing as they have been steadily doing for many years.

With the mention of J. F. K, one must give question to his actual assassination.
There have been many words written and spoken concerning the assassination of J. F. K and those responsible for his death, so it will not be dwelt on in major detail here. One name mentioned above all others and in greatest association with the assignation, is that of Lee Harvey Oswald. It is not being asserted here that Oswald did not have a part to play in the proceeding, but with the evidence that is available for even the most closed minded of people, his participation in and assassination of J. F. K is most definitely brought into question.

Let us address but a few simple points that it would appear that the Warren commission either over-looked or purposely did not include in the findings of the report.
Upon entering the book repository and undertaking a very quick search, the police found four empty cartridge casings from the Carcano M91/38 bolt-action rifle supposedly found at the scene. These empty casings had been lined up nice and neatly next to each other on the window ledge. The casings being left at the scene and being lined so neatly, just does not make any sense. If Oswald had been the shooter, then why would he have left valuable evidence that could have convicted him, such as the empty casings? Any realistically sensible assassin would have taken the casings with them. Any spent casings would have been scooped up and placed into a pocket or somewhere safe to be disposed of later. Something mentioned a little earlier concerns the finding of Oswald's rifle in a corner of the same room as the bullet casings. One of the first responders, a police officer by the name of Sheriff's Deputy Roger Craig, stated that the markings

on the rifle found, stamped clearly on the barrel were 7.62 Mauser. Obviously this does not make any sense at all no matter how one twists it around. Why did the responding officers find a 7.62 Mauser, yet the Warren commission reported that the rifle that was used was a Carcano M91/38?

Here we come to a major point. Why was the rifle that was supposedly used, left at the scene? There are several possibilities;
Firstly, the shooter was just totally incompetent and had no idea what they were doing and made things up ad hoc. This does not hold water as an answer. For anyone to carry out the act they must have had the ability to get weapons, find a position that would be advantageous from which to shoot and calmly fire four shots before hiding the rifle behind some boxes in the same room, after which they left. These actions point to an individual who would have been calm, collected, productive and ruthless in their actions. An individual of this type would most certainly not leave the rifle or the empty casings behind to be easily found by the police.

Secondly, it could be argued that the shooter, allegedly Lee Harvey Oswald, wanted to be caught. That he was mentally unstable and therefore wanted his moment of fame or infamy. Again, this as an answer does not hold water. If he was the shooter and wanted to get caught, then there is no doubt that he would have admitted killing the president, a fact that he denied. Also, rather than shooting from a position that was in effect hidden, he would have committed the shooting from a position where he could have been clearly seen; as with the reduced levels of security at the time, this would have been more than possible.

Thirdly, the final possibility is that Lee Harvey Oswald was arrested and blamed for the shooting of President J. F. Kennedy to cover for those who actually sanctioned the assassination and those who committed the act. In other words Lee Harvey Oswald was used as a 'patsy' by those whose interests would be firmly rooted in the permanent removal of the President from office.

One fascinating point with regard to the assassination of President J. F. Kennedy that must be focused on is that of the final blow, the shot that actually killed the President. One should bear in mind that Lee Harvey Oswald was said to have fired the killing blow from a window of the book depository. This means that he could only have shot the President from behind. Yet when viewing the film that was recorded at the exact moment that the final shot hit the President, the President's body moves sharply back and slightly to the left as he is hit in the head by a projectile.

Unless the laws of the physical world we live in changed for a few seconds just as the bullet left the barrel of the weapon, thus allowing the bullet to be fired in a forward direction and then turn itself around almost 180^0, then President Kennedy was shot in the head and killed by a bullet fired from the front and not the back as is the official version of events. Therefore Lee Harvey Oswald could not have fired the bullet that actually killed the President.

Compounding evidence for a shot fired from the front and perhaps slightly to the right of the President, is that of a Police motorcyclist Bobby Hargis who was travelling with the President's motor cade and riding behind and to the left of the President's car. The Police officer was to have blood and brain matter covering part of his uniform as a result of the head shot received by the President. If the shot had been fired from behind the president, then it would be very unlikely that the officer could, given his position relative to the President' motorcade, have come in contact with any blood or other matter from the President's shooting. Officer Hargis stated, "Then I felt something hit me. It could have been concrete or something, but I thought at first I might have been hit." If the police officer thought that he might have been struck by something as hard as concrete, then the physical matter that struck him must have been moving with considerable force. Which once again is suggestive of a shot being fired at President Kennedy from the front rather than from the rear.

There is much, much more that could be said about President Kennedy's assassination; the views of Dr. Charles Crenshaw who was working at the Parkland Hospital, Dallas. The supposed change of caskets in which Kennedy's body was placed. Possible damage to the area of the head wound, post factum. The views and evidence of Police officers on duty at the time.

But for now only one more point will be added. In an article printed by the Telegraph, titled, "Oswald had no time to fire all Kennedy bullets." It states that tests carried out under the supervision of the Italian army with a Mannlicher-Carcano bolt-action rifle, the same model of rifle that the Warren commission stated was the weapon used by Oswald to assassinate President Kennedy, showed that it was impossible for Oswald to have carried out the action;

"The official Warren Commission inquiry into the shooting concluded the following year that Oswald was a lone gunman who fired three shots with a Carcano M91/38 bolt-action rifle in 8.3 seconds..."
"But when the Italian team test-fired the identical model of gun, they were unable to load and fire three shots in less than 19 seconds..."
"...it was found to be impossible for even an accomplished marksman to fire the shots quickly enough."

Tim Shipman, Telegraph. 01 Jul 2007

It would appear that a number of serious events were either ignored or omitted by those in charge of the Warren Commission. When the evidence of the whole situation is put together, the official version of events as set out by the Warren commission does, to put it mildly, leave a lot to be desired.

A Large False Flag?

The best place to hide something is in plain sight. There has been much controversy concerning the collapse of the two towers of the world trade centre, building 7 and also the damage done to the Pentagon on 11th September, 2001. Although it is doubtful that there is anyone alive today that is not aware of what happened on that sad day, it will be covered quickly here, just in case there might be some who are not aware of what took place.

On 11th September 2001, a number of terrorists took control of four passenger jets over American air space. Two of the aircraft were forced to fly into the two towers of the World Trade Centre, one was flown into the Pentagon and on board the fourth passenger jet, the passengers attempted to take back control from the terrorists, the result of this was that the aircraft crashed into a field in Stonycreek Township near Shanksville, Pennsylvania. Due to the actions of the terrorists on that day, thousands of people in the world trade centre, staff at the Pentagon and all of the passengers and crew on each of the four passenger planes died. This was one of the worst terrorist actions in history.

It is sometimes a good idea to put to one side the official findings of an event and look at the actual reality of a situation, by doing this one can avoid being led by the nose through events and situations where others choose what the public should or should not believe. One should not blindly follow the narrative that any governmentally funded body delivers as being the whole truth. This is not to say that all governmentally funded bodies are easily influenced by those funding them, as there are those whose honesty and principles are above reproach. People should look at the information available and weigh up the possibilities and probabilities of events taking place as officially stated.

According to the official narrative, on the 11th of September 2001 four passenger planes were taken over by terrorists and used in a devastating attack upon the American people.
Two of the planes were flown into the two towers of the World Trade Centre in New York. This action was the cause of fires breaking out in both of the towers, which was officially the cause of their collapse after a very short period of time.

Many articles have been written concerning the events of this day, some follow the official narrative, whilst others dispute the government's version of events and the reason for the collapses, so there isn't much one can say other than focus on a small number of points. If one addresses what actually happened on the day in question, then there is no doubt that the official account does leave much that should be questioned.

Of the terrorists supposedly on the particular flights that were named by the American government, a number of them were and most possibly still are alive and well and living in their own countries. Saeed Al-Ghamdi, 25, a Saudi Airlines pilot and Abdulaziz Al-Omari, an engineer, are just two of the reported terrorists. Neither of these two men had anything to do with the terrorist actions on 9/11. In fact they were not even in America at the time. The same can be said of a number of other men reported by the American security services as being among the 9/11 terrorists. Yet their personal details were laid open to the public world-wide, alongside the accusations of committing horrendous crimes.

This is something that should be of serious concern as the American security services did not only get things wrong, but released the details of individuals who had nothing to do with the situation. One should at this point question how something like this could happen. Perhaps names were just pulled from a hat! This does seem to be a distinct possibility, either that or the security services were so incompetent that one wonders how they manage to function at all. There is another possibility, that of the whole situation being staged and that the majority of the American security services whilst being very good at their jobs were ignorant of the false flag that took place.

When watching film of one of the two towers collapsing, the top section of one of the towers leans over severely to one side. Now, according to the laws of the physical world that we live within, the top section should have continued to fall following the line of least resistance, in other words, continuing to fall in the same direction, with its own energy increasing its momentum thus carrying it forward. This would have meant that the top section of the building would have fallen as one complete block until coming in contact with either the ground or some other building. Yet this did not happen, instead, the whole massive block appeared to disintegrate in mid-air and fall straight down. Again, the official account seems to be lacking in evidential truth. The falling section obviously did not succumb to fire, it should have crashed to the ground causing massive damage to other buildings in the surrounding area below.

Both of the towers fell, one shortly after the other, disintegrating as they plummeted ground-ward. This in itself is amazing and should give serious concern as to the safety and strength of any tall building. There have been many very tall buildings around the world that have suffered substantial fires, yet amazingly they did not collapse nor did they disintegrate. It should be mentioned that when both of the towers collapsed, they fell straight down causing limited damage to the surrounding buildings. They fell almost into their own footprints.

The vehicles in a wide area surrounding the collapsed towers were burnt. It could be thought that they were burnt by the fire that supposedly consumed the towers, but this cannot be the case. The reason it is not possible is quite simple, if the fire from the towers had been sufficient to badly burn vehicles, then it would also have been sufficient to set other buildings alight, thus causing massive multi-block fires all around the area. This did not happen.

There were numerous reports of explosions coming from the two towers prior to their collapse from fire crews and members of the public. These reports were ignored and/or explained away, assuming that the public are generally stupid enough to forget what they have seen with their own eyes and heard with their own ears.
Let us move forward a little to an interesting comment made by the then National Security Advisor, Condoleezza Rice,

"I don't think anybody could have predicted that they would try to use an airplane as a missile, a hijacked airplane as a missile."

(16th May, 2002, National Security
Adviser Condoleezza Rice)

This comment should raise at least a little concern as, if one reads a document named *'Operation Northwoods'*, headed, 'Joint Chiefs of Staff' and dated 13th March 1962, one can clearly see that with regard to the bad relations between the United States and Cuba, the American military came up with numerous ideas and methods to gain justification through public backing for going to war with Cuba. Just one of these methods was to paint and number an aircraft to appear as an exact copy of a civil registered aircraft, yet the aircraft used would belong to a 'CIA proprietary organisation',
1.   The aircraft would then be boarded by passengers with "...carefully prepared aliases"
2. The original civil registered aircraft would be turned into a drone.   Both planes would meet at unspecified airborne coordinates where the drone would be destroyed and the plane carrying the prepared passengers would land at an unspecified location. This would make it appear that Cuban forces had shot down a passenger plane, thus enflaming the American public and ensuring that they would accept military action and intervention.

One is forced to ask, that if the American government were prepared if necessary to go to these lengths in 1962, then to what lengths would it go to ensure war with Iraq? If morally dubious members of the bureaucracy had the capacity to enable the enactment of such a repugnant scheme in 1962, then what could such people have been capable of dreaming up in 2001, given the advancement in technology?

There is much, much more that could be said concerning the collapse of the World trade Centre, and many books that have been written concerning the matter, however, perhaps the words below would give greater food for thought and open minds to the possibility of larger governmental machinations that might and often do take place.

> *"It is easier to fool people than convince them they have been fooled."*

Saying attributed to Mark Twain.

Finally, the situation was immediately designated as a terrorist attack, this negated the possibility of any criminal investigation. So the official narrative was the only one to which members of the public could possibly have access.

Politics and Politicians

The job/position of modern politician is one that socially allows an individual or group of individuals of like-minded social views (political party) to affect and influence the lives of others within their society. Invariably, although not in all cases, the individual or political party profit considerably in one way or another at the expense of the population.

To take up the mantle of a politician one must without doubt have an elevated ego and over indulgent sense of self-importance. In some cases this will not necessarily be a bad thing, although it would appear that in the vast majority of cases, the individual's ego far out-weighs their abilities. One only has to look through history and modern history in particular to see the damage that politics and politicians have caused. The words and actions of politicians have cost the lives of so many, causing such heart ache for friends and family that one can only imagine how God must weep.

Contrary to popular opinion (well, the opinion of the political class), the world would function perfectly well without politicians. In fact it would run rather nicely. It is the political class and their sycophantic devotees that practice their convoluted machinations, fundamentally causing the vast majority of wars in the world. The general population of the world would live perfectly happy, enjoyable lives without the artificially created 'profession' of politics.

The populations are persuaded by governments that politicians are a necessary and vital component of society, and so albeit begrudgingly, people accept this supposedly necessary social evil into their lives. Morality and ethical standards are human traits that appear to be distinctly lacking within most governmental bodies insofar as, it is governments that decide on a particular course of action, one that invariably is not to the advantage of those that they supposedly represent. What appears to take place is that the political class and those associated with this class, profit, literally or metaphorically, from a given decision or action at the expense of the population.

The population are manipulated to believe that they need what governments tell them they need. Propaganda pours forth from the mouths of politicians as a bovine excreting, having digested something that turned out to be rather unpalatable. All the while, the mainstream media produce what can only be described as 'Fake' news to bolster the governments chosen paths. The vast majority of the population, although not necessarily through stupidity, ingest the propaganda. The population fall in line like sheep to slaughter. One cannot help but wonder if sheep look at the human race and laugh.

When put altogether this must seem like a damming indictment of the political class, and so it is, although as stated earlier, it relates to the majority of politicians, not all. There will always be a limited number of politicians who genuinely do attempt to work for the benefit of their constituents and the population as a whole.

Something that should without doubt be mentioned, is the matter of the British 'Brexit'. In 2016 the British government held a national referendum for the population to decide whether to stay in the E.U, (European Union) or to leave it. The majority of the population voted to exit the E.U. Since the results of the referendum were announced the British government dithered and prevaricated with regard to the matter of triggering Article 50 of the Lisbon Treaty. Finally, after a court case that was brought about through the actions of a very disgruntled woman (who will not be named here) who just happened to be in favour of staying in the E.U, it was decided that the British government should have the final vote with regard to the matter of either staying in or leaving the E. U.

Two points of interest should be raised here: Firstly, that the woman who instigated the court case has shown that she has absolutely no regard for the opinions of others, and that she obviously holds the supposed democratic process within the U.K in complete contempt. By taking a court action in this way, she has shown that instead of following the democratic process in that the majority make the decisions, she has shown a petulance that would not be out of place in a kindergarten.

Secondly and more importantly is the fact that politicians were going to be permitted to vote in the British parliament with regard to the matter of leaving or staying in the E.U. They seem to have forgotten, as have the majority of politicians around the world, that they are in the positions they hold to do what the population want them to do, and not the other way around. The arrogance of these people is almost unbelievable. They had completely ignored the fact that they had already voted with regard to this matter, on the same day as the rest of the population. Just because something does not go the way that you want, you do not disregard the wishes of the people. It should be remembered that politicians are simply the servants of the people, although this fact seems to be lost on the vast majority of politicians, whose sense of self-importance far out-weighs their abilities.

Distribution of Power and Wealth

There have and always will be those who crave wealth and those who desire power.
There is nothing wrong with being wealthy, it is something that in this world the majority of people work towards. In essence, all wealth does for anyone is permit them to lead more enjoyable lives. Wealth allows an individual a greater perception of independence and creativity, also, better food, better healthcare and a better education are among the many positives that wealth can enable. There is one point with regard to wealth that never ceases to rear its ugly head and that is the misguided perception that greater wealth equals greater intelligence. But, wealth does not and cannot give an individual greater intelligence.
As mentioned earlier a better standard of education can be gained, but it should be remembered that contradicting popular belief, education and intelligence are not synonymous. No matter how hard the intransigent elements in the realm of psychology disagree, an individual's level of intelligence cannot be determined by tests, (intelligence quotient). One may spend vast amounts of money on education, thus gaining knowledge of much in the way of supposed facts, but this does not and will not make one intelligent. It should be noted that intelligence is relative. The simplest way of explaining this would be to say that intelligence is quite simply; how one applies the knowledge one has within the particular environment that one finds oneself in, at any given moment in time.

Perhaps giving an example would make this a little clearer:
Let us view a situation where a business man or woman takes a flight from France to Peru. The flight suffers engine failure and comes to earth somewhere in the Amazon rain forest. Our business man or woman is the only person to walk away from the wreckage. Now let us assume for the sake of argument, that this person has been educated at the finest of schools and progressed on to higher education. Having passed through the education processes at one of the greatest universities, this individual

should have gained considerable knowledge of both the subjects that they have studied, and also achieved a wide base of general knowledge throughout their journey. Their voyage through the education system will have, without doubt, cost hundreds of thousands of dollars or pounds.

In our hypothetical plane crash scenario, intelligence for the business man or woman is simple; applying the knowledge that they have gained over many years to survive, even if only for a short time. The important factors in our scenario are: finding a suitable shelter, making a fire and obtaining food and water.

Intelligence has a closer proximity to common sense than it does to having been through the education system, no matter how much money has been spent on that education. What is the point of our example? Well, in the safe environment within which our business man or woman would usually function, they would consider themselves highly intelligent due to their education and the amount of money that they have been able to accumulate due to this education. Yet, when placed into a real situation in life they would with little doubt struggle to survive, if managing to cope at all. Intelligence is therefore relative. Yet surprisingly enough, society appears to be of the unspoken opinion that intelligence is gained through standard education. Status within society is generally based on one's financial success. So both intelligence and social status are based on inconsequential factors.

Yet surprisingly enough, the population of any country misguidedly hands control of their lives over to people whose only claim to have the abilities necessary to know what is best for the people, is that of having been through a somewhat dubious education system. One should bear in mind that the education system teaches the information that the elite dictate. This information follows the dogma that keeps the elite in their lofty positions, usually at the expense both financially and economically of the very populations that they are supposedly there to help. The population often and without hesitation absorb the propaganda poured forth, wholly unaware of their blunder.

The people have given away the power over their very lives to individuals who are following their own agenda. At such an accusation, voices in government would cry out in anguished argument and indignation, "Rules and laws are created for the betterment of all." If only that were true. The majority of laws ensure the population remains subdued, keeping them from the realization that both they and their children are in effect the property of the state and therefore of the elite. This undoubtedly sounds distinctly Orwellian, as indeed it is, until one looks deeper into the rabbit hole.

The control of the elite is so extensive in its reach that it has the capability to take a country to war, even though that act be against the wishes of the general population, as was the case with the British Prime Minister Tony Blair. Mr. Blair, if one is not already acquainted with the circumstances, took the British people to war allied with the United States of America, against the middle eastern country of Iraq. The reason for this action was, according to Mr. Blair, to stop the Iraqi leader Saddam Hussain from producing weapons of mass destruction, primarily the creation of nuclear weapons. Mr. Blair persuaded the western world that Saddam Hussain could execute an attack against countries in the western hemisphere using weapons of mass destruction and also carry out the said strike within just a forty-five minute window. The majority of members of the British parliament allowed themselves to be persuaded by the supposed veracity of Blair's statement to parliament regarding the matter, without finding out the facts for themselves. The British Government duly sanctioned the war.

One member of the House of Commons who rejected Blair's demand for war, was Mr. Robin Cooke. Not only did Robin Cooke reject Blair's desire for war, but he stood firm upon his principles and beliefs, resigning from government. Through his actions, Robin Cook showed himself to be one of the greatest politicians of his age, and one of the rarest of all things in the world of politics, an honest and trustworthy human being.

One man who was aware that Iraq did not have the military capability that Blair declared to the British parliament with regard to weapons of mass destruction, was weapons inspector Dr. David Kelly. Dr. David Kelly, according to the Hutton report, took his own life by ingesting tablets and cutting his wrists. His supposed suicide took place just prior to him preparing to leave the country to continue his work in Iraq.

It is a damming indictment of any government that a respectable individual such as Dr. David Kelly who was working for that government was found dead, supposedly by suicide, having stated that in his opinion there were no weapons of mass destruction, just at the time when the government had gone to war using weapons of mass destruction as the justification for such an action. It could easily be considered that perhaps Dr Kelly's untimely death was rather convenient to say the least. Interestingly, the Hutton inquiry was not a statutory inquiry and had far less legal powers than an inquest and as such Lord Hutton could not make witnesses give evidence under oath. Yet Lord Hutton did it would appear, have the power and authority to ensure that information relating to the supposed suicide will remain hidden from the public for no less than 70 years.

There are numerous professional individuals who have been seeking a full inquest into the death of Dr David Kelly to take place, even after so many years have passed.   Dr. Michael Powers QC, confirmed to the Mail on Sunday newspaper, that he had seen a letter, written by Nick Graham, who at the time was assistant head of legal and democratic services Oxford council, stating that unusual restrictions had been placed by Lord Hutton on material relating to his inquiry,

"Lord Hutton made a request for the records provided to the inquiry, not produced in evidence, to be closed for 30 years, and that medical (including post-mortem) reports and photographs be closed for 70 years."

The Telegraph, Wednesday 17th 2017, (Mail on Sunday, 24 Jan 2010)

A good man died so that Tony Blair could have his war and continue the move forward by the globalists. Perhaps note should be taken that Saddam Hussain did use chemical weaponry against the Kurdish population in the north of Iraq, an evil and unforgivable act. But how many people are actually aware of who supplied these weapons. If one examines the question of who supplied these weapons, the answer found should disgust any truly caring human being.

People have had their rights eroded by the wealthy and the powerful. Those 'at the top' have allowed their egos to run riot, their arrogance knowing no bounds, affecting all areas of life from virtual censorship to G.M.O's (Genetically Modified Organism). The saddest of all realizations is that the population of the world actually believe what the oligarchs say, blindly following whatever idiocy the elite decide upon.

One other section of our modern society that can and often does have a profound effect on the views and beliefs of a population is the sphere of celebrities. All people are entitled to their personal views, whatever they are, with the proviso that no harm is caused either directly or indirectly by those views. Yet many of those supposed celebrities appear to be of the opinion that they can make statements publicly, statements that could have devastating results. An example of this would be the singer and actress Madonna. Madonna informed a large crowd that was demonstrating in America, that she had been thinking about 'Blowing up the White House'. This was not mentioned just once, but stated a number of times. Firstly, the notion of 'Blowing up the White house' is one of the most idiotic ideas that one could have. Secondly and of vastly more importance is the fact that, committing such an act could without any doubt be the spark that brings about either the horror of a civil war in the United States or something of a greater magnitude, it could fuel the flames for a vastly more significant event, a third world war. There are all kinds of extremists in this world and such words spoken by a prominent, although somewhat ignorant individual, could encourage any extremist to either carry out an action of this sort, or attempt to.

Having said this, there has been a rise in people around the world awakening from their state of almost unconsciousness acquiescence. Some people have begun to query what they have been taught from birth, questioning the disingenuous elite and demanding both answers and change. The more people have been made aware of alternative information, the more they have looked deeper in to the history of the world and likewise domestic events, thus, the greater the number of 'conspiracy theorists' has become. Being accused of being a conspiracy theorist was for many years a method by which the elite could keep the truth from surfacing. The mocking attitudes shown toward those who question the official explanations of countless events is no longer enough to keep control of information dissemination. With more and more people world-wide questioning the official narrative with regard to numerous subjects and events, the patronising and condescending attitude shown by the elite is no longer sufficient to keep people in the required delusionary state that can be relatively easily controlled.

Fake news and a World of Conspiracies

In late 2016 and early 2017 the term 'Fake News' came to the forefront of society, thrust forward by a media that is to a large extent owned by or connected closely to an elite and controlling element of our society. In a simple but clever move, the establishment has begun to avoid the term 'conspiracy theory' and as an alternative introduced the term 'Fake News'. This simple change in wording may not seem at first glance to be of any real significance, but when one looks a little deeper, this change in terminology may well have fateful ramifications for the future of freedom of speech in the western hemisphere.

Up until the present day it has been relatively easy for governments and the world elite to limit undesirable information from flowing out to the general population, information that would or might prove wrong-doing or bring into question the validity of the official narrative. Anyone questioning the official version of events with regard to a given subject or event could be easily labelled as a 'Conspiracy Theorist'. On these occasions the term 'Conspiracy Theorist' has been used in a derogatory way whereby an individual or group can and do lose credibility, consequently being regarded as the 'fringe element' of society. Yet, as greater numbers of people are waking up from their propaganda fuelled reverie, the term 'Conspiracy Theorist' is quickly losing its negative connotations. To fill the vacuum that will undoubtedly arise from being unable to socially label this undesirable element, the term 'Fake News' was conceived.

One might wonder, what is 'Fake News'? Fake news is quite simply, false information. Material that will often have some sensational quality associated with it. Such information is disseminated, often world-wide through the guise of being factual and based on reality. There will always be what can only be described as 'genuine' fake news. Certain elements of the media as a matter of course have and will sensationalise stories, some will even go so far as to create a news items out of thin air to ensure sales. There are also many cases where individuals will themselves create a fiction just for their fifteen minutes of fame. Numerous other similar instances of such types of behaviour exist across the world. This having been said, it is not only the media and sections of the population that produce fake news. Fake news is a wonderful gift for governments and also for the military industrial complex mentioned by President Eisenhower.

Fake news is, when manipulated by those in power, just propaganda by another name. There will always in any society be those that refuse under any circumstances to accept that their government, or an elite element within society constantly manipulate the people, the laws and the financial institutions to their own ends. But all too often this is the case and has been through-out time, particularly in the twentieth and twenty-first centuries.

Fake news in 1964.

In 1964 the United States of America did in effect finally enter into war with North Vietnam. The western world was at that time still gripped with the fear of communist expansionism, and there were more than underlying fears that South-Eastern Asia might succumb to the 'evils' of communism. With this in mind and the ongoing conflict between North and South Vietnam favouring the North, the United States under President Lyndon Johnson made the decision that military intervention was the necessary course to take. To undertake an action such as putting the United States on a path to war, the administration would need suitable justification to gain the support of congress and more importantly the American public. For many years the American people had sensibly been somewhat reserved in their position regarding both the idea and the act of going to war.
American opinion had, prior to both world war one and world war two, adopted a policy of neutrality and isolation, prudently entrenched in the view of non-interventionism. On each of these occasions America was drawn into war by the administration and

the elite of the time manipulating events to suit their own ends. To facilitate their involvement in the ongoing Vietnamese conflict and stop South-Eastern Asia from supposedly falling under the yolk of communism, the administration needed once again to manipulate events.

The Bay of Tonkin incident:

On August 5, 1964, a Washington post news item, stated,
"American Planes Hit North Vietnam After Second Attack on Our Destroyers; Move Taken to Halt New Aggression."

Washington post, August 5, 1964.

On the same day The New York Times reported that,
"President Johnson has ordered retaliatory action against gunboats and supporting facilities in North Vietnam after renewed attacks against American destroyers in the Gulf of Tonkin."

New York Times, August 5, 1964.

The fact is that the above statements were neither entirely accurate nor true. This by definition would make these statements 'Fake News'!
The leadership of the United States at the time gave the official version of events as follows; on the 2nd of August, North Vietnamese torpedo boats initiated an 'unprovoked attack' against the U.S. destroyer Maddox whilst on a routine patrol. Two days later on the night of the 4th of August, a second attack took place against United States naval forces. This second attack again involved North Vietnamese PT boats (patrol torpedo boats) following up with a 'deliberate attack' against two U.S ships in the Tonkin Gulf.

The known facts show a different version of events. On the 2nd Of August, the U.S.S Maddox (Figure. 9) was carrying out aggressive intelligence-gathering maneuvers. These aggressive intelligence-gathering maneuvers were undertaken in conjunction with attacks by the South Vietnamese navy and the Laotian air force against North Vietnam, something which the administration and the press both conveniently neglected to mention.

Fig.9

USS Maddox

Huffpost, The worldpost, 2017.

The 4th of August attack did not it would appear, even take place. U.S. task force commander, Captain John J. Herrick made reference to *"freak weather effects"*, *"almost total darkness"* and also a sonar operator who was perhaps somewhat overeager in his duties and who *"was hearing the ship's own propeller beat."* Squadron commander James Stockdale was a Navy pilot and airborne on the night in question, he stated,

"I had the best seat in the house to watch that event...," he continued, *"...and our destroyers were just shooting at phantom targets — there were no PT boats there.... There was nothing there but black water and American fire power."*

FAIR. Fair.org/

Had the truth been released by the administration and if the press had shown any professional integrity and honesty in doing their jobs, then an estimated 58,220 American service personnel would have had the chance to live long and fruitful lives.
There is not a solid number for the total loss of Vietnamese lives caused by the conflict, although general consensus puts

estimates at between 2-3 million persons. There can be no accounting for the suffering, the anguish, the sorrow and the pain that was caused on both sides due to the desire for power and money by those faceless oligarchs of the military industrial complex.

Theoretically, reputable reporters should be above blindly following the wants and desires of their 'lords and masters', but as is often the case, the administration dictates, directly or indirectly, what should go to press, immaterial of accuracy of fact. It must be pointed out that the above is not the case with all reporters, although it does seem that the majority of those in the press will follow whatever falsehood they are directed to follow.

The expediency of 'Fake News'.

In 2003, Britain and America went to war in Iraq. The reason given was simple, that President Saddam Hussain was in possession of weapons of mass destruction. Prime Minister Tony Blair emphasised to the British parliament on 24th September 2002 that these weapons of mass destruction, including chemical weapons could be activated within forty-five minutes. The notification of a forty-five minute activation window was something that was to have a profound effect on the minds and reactions of millions of people. This statement of the relatively short period required for activation of these weapons was something that was noted and pursued by the press and the general public. The specifics surrounding this stated time period were neither elaborated on nor stressed by the Prime Minister Tony Blair. The continued emphasis of the forty-five minute period by the press was later noted by Tony Blair when questioned at the Iraq inquiry. He also noted that in hindsight it would been better to have corrected this statement,

> *"...in light of the significance it later took on".*
>
> Tony Blair, Iraq Inquiry

This information was so we are told given by the intelligence services to the Prime Minister. So this would imply that the intelligence services either gave incorrect information to the Prime Minister, or that they did not give a correct interpretation of the meaning of the activation time given. To assert either of the above to be true, would be to 'pass the buck'. (Something it seems politicians do the world over). The security services did their jobs, gathering information to the best of their abilities and stating as accurately as possible the facts as they appeared. This information was then directly passed on to the heads of governments. Yet, when Tony Blair addressed the British government regarding the matter he did not specify, as was the case, that the forty-five minute period was in relation to Iraq and the neighbouring geographical area. The public like-wise were not told of any distinction, leaving the populations under the impression that they could be attacked in their own countries within a period of forty-five minutes. Saddam Hussain did not at the time possess a delivery system capable of striking either Britain or America. This is something that would have been known by all of the security services at the time and therefore also by both governments and also by Mr Blair.

Although Tony Blair acknowledged that in hindsight he should have corrected his statement regarding the matter of the forty-five minutes, instead he took the course of 'passing the buck' onto the shoulders of both the security services and the press for inaccurately reporting or misinterpreting the facts.

"In the House of Commons on 18 March 2003, Mr Blair stated that he judged the possibility of terrorist groups in possession of WMD was "a real and present danger to Britain and its national security" – and that the threat from Saddam Hussein's arsenal could not be contained and posed a clear danger to British citizens."

Statement by Sir John Chilcot: 6 July 2016

This just cannot be the case. Mr Blair was fully conversant with the reports of the security services and as such he would have been aware at the time of the major distinction to which that the forty-five minute period referred. Also, with the enormity of the decisions laid out before him and the resources at his disposal, one would have thought that a British Prime Minister would have examined each and every detail and given a true and accurate representation of the facts at the time. Instead, certain details as mentioned above, were omitted.   The only reasonable assumption that can be drawn from this is that the omission by the Prime Minster to the general public of particular details would be to expedite a clear path to war with Iraq. By not correcting information at the time, Mr Blair permitted the use of 'fake news' to perpetuate a falsehood that would cause numerous deaths and incalculable suffering.

Interestingly enough on the 28th September 2004, Mr Blair stated at a labour conference that the intelligence regarding weapons of mass destruction had been incorrect. Again, the security services were said to be at fault.

Perhaps at this point one should question the legitimacy of Mr Blair's reasons for taking the British people to war in a distant country that was of no direct threat to the British people. As was found to be the case, there were no weapons of mass destruction, the forty-five minute weapons activation time as was implied by Tony Blair to the government and the people was a gross misrepresentation of the truth, and the interpretation of the United Nations resolution 1441 was dubious to say the least. He decided also to ignore leading figures such as Hans Blix, the head of the United Nations Monitoring, Verification and Inspection Commission at the time, and Kofi Annan, United Nations secretary general, instead, Mr Blair insisted on pursuing the war in Iraq.

Sir John Chilcot did later, in what was to be known as the 'Chilcot report' state:

> *"We have concluded that the UK chose to join the invasion of Iraq before the peaceful options for disarmament had been exhausted. Military action at that time was not a last resort."*
>
> Statement by Sir John Chilcot: 6 July 2016

This should lead one to ask the question, that if the supposed threat did not exist at the time as stated, then why would a war with Iraq be necessary?

There is no doubt that Saddam Hussain as portrayed was not a very pleasant individual. It is not disputed that, as we are told, he committed crimes against his own people including the detainment, torture and killing of citizens of his own country. The ill-treatment of the Kurdish population of Iraq can never be excused and such treatment of people anywhere in the world should always be condemned. Although Saddam Hussain was said to be guilty of such crimes, these crimes were never given as the reason for the invasion of Iraq, as has been discussed earlier, the reasons were, whether legal or not, completely different. Given as pointed out earlier that the reasons submitted by Prime Minister Tony Blair had insufficient foundation for an invasion, the only other reasonable assumption that can be made is that of regime change. This is not as farfetched as it may sound.

On September 28th 2004, at a Labour conference, Mr Blair having confessed that the 'intelligence' was inaccurate, changed track with regard to the Iraq regime change, presenting regime change itself as justification for the war. According to the BBC, Mr Blair stated,

> *"I can apologise for the information being wrong, but I can never apologise, sincerely at least, for removing Saddam. The world is a better place with Saddam in prison not in power."*
>
> BBC, news.bbc.co.uk/1/hi/uk_politics

51

On the 1st of May 2005, it was reported:

"A leaked memo suggested that Mr Blair was looking at ways to justify war with Iraq in July 2002, but he told the BBC that was wrong - despite his previous claims that regime change was morally right."

"If the UN resolution had been adhered to by Saddam that would have been the end of it, despite the fact it was the most appalling regime".

Tony Blair, BBC, news.bbc.co.uk/1/hi/uk_politics

12 December 2009, while being interviewed by Fern Brittan from the BBC, Mr Blair stated the following, "

"...a lack of WMD would not have saved Saddam: I would still have thought it right to remove him. I mean obviously you would have had to use and deploy different arguments about the nature of the threat." Mr Blair continued, saying, *"The 'notion' of Saddam as a threat was what mattered, and one aspect of that was 'the development of WMD'."*

Tony Blair, BBC, news.bbc.co.uk/1/hi/uk_politics

Mr Blair claimed that it was important to be operating in accordance with international law. Yet as has been seen already, the Iraq war was indisputably and unequivocally illegal.

If Mr Blair was so set on staying under the umbrella of international law, then why did he manipulate the interpretation of U.N resolution 1441 to suit his own ends and also, (and perhaps of more importance), why did he keep referring to regime change. Under international law, regime change cannot be addressed as a final goal and using war to facilitate regime change in this fashion is wholly illegal under international law. It would seem that Mr Blair's supposed desire to stay within international law was not based in reality.

Before the final step to war is taken, many things need to be addressed, tactics need to be drawn up, targets assigned and logistical concerns focused upon, and there must also be an 'end game' in place. There must be plans laid out to ensure the

52

continued and effective running of a country's infrastructure to ensure the well-being of the subjugated population. In the case of Iraq,   something that recent history has shown, is that this simply was not the case.

Since the Iraq war the country of Iraq and the surrounding geographical area has fallen into the abyss. Hundreds of thousands, if not millions of men, women and children have died as a consequence of the war. Numerous allied service personal suffered and or died needlessly, leaving their families with a void in their lives which was once filled by their loved ones. It would be easy to say that the horror that was unleased upon Iraq and its population both during and more importantly since the war could not have been foreseen, but to follow that line of thought would be naïve and purposely avoid facing the truth. The instigators of the war would have been fully conversant with the probabilities of the political and social upheaval and eventual collapse that followed. Intelligence services world-wide are constantly monitoring the stability of governmental systems and ongoing political scheming, and will without doubt inform their superiors, and so the figures 'at the top' were well aware of what would most likely happen. The entire region of the Middle East suffered severe destabilisation, finally culminating in the rise of the terrorist group known as ISIS. The effects of this deterioration had a dramatic effect on the neighbouring country of Syria, sending it spiralling into a horrendous civil war.
The result of the Gulf war has, in the long run, had colossal repercussions world-wide. Culpability rests squarely on the shoulders of those few individuals who without legal justification, took their countries to war, but it also rests on the shoulders of those powerful oligarchs who lurk in the background, unseen, pulling the strings of and misleading populations to suit their own ends.

Destabilisation and Manipulation

There have been and still are a number of regimes around the world who undertake crimes no less horrific than committed by Saddam Hussain, yet Ex British Prime Minster Mr Tony Blair has not desired war as a solution to end their crimes. There are numerous countries that have weapons of mass destruction and might not be regarded as the most stable of political elements; again there has been no desire for the removal of their political leadership. Perhaps at this point one should ask why only certain countries have been and are being the target of forced regime removal, either directly or allegedly through covert involvement.

Retired United States General Wesley Clark, (Figure. 10) in an interview with 'Democracy Now!' host Amy Goodman offered an insight into the minds of the powerful lunatic fringe of this world. In the interview he stated that he was told by a pentagon insider, just days after the 9/11 attack, that America was going to war with Iraq. Iraq and its leadership did not have anything to do with the horrific attack carried out by terrorists under the direction of Al-Qaeda's commander Osama Bin Laden, yet a connection was created nonetheless. This connection was not based on evidential fact, but on the desire of an elite to undermine stability in the Middle-East. Why would anyone in their right mind desire to create fractures in an area that was already volatile? With the Middle-East already teetering on a knife edge, surely anyone of sound mine and who had at least the slightest humanity would address the notion of peace, even though that peace be strained. This was not to be the case.

General Wesley Clark in his interview with Amy Goodman, gave more than just the information on the invasion of Iraq. He stated that in November of 2001, a senior military staff officer at the pentagon expanded on the earlier information saying that Iraq was being discussed,

Fig.10

General Wesley Clark (Retired)

"...as part of a five-year campaign plan, ...and there were a total of seven countries, beginning with Iraq, then Syria, Lebanon, Libya, Iran, Somalia and Sudan..."

Gen. Wesley Clark, Winning Modern Wars, 2003.

Were it not for the fact that these words came from a respected United States General, then they would appear laughable. That these words were spoken of with regard to the administration in power at the time, should raise grave concerns to anyone who believes in the principles of freedom and justice. But why would these countries be the targets of American military and industrial might? That is not a question to which one can find the answer and substantiate that answer with concrete fact, given that so much information is classified under the umbrella of National Security. When material is finally realised into the public domain under the freedom of information act, it is so heavily redacted as to make it almost, if not in some cases completely indecipherable. So what can be done to answer the above question of why would these countries be the targets of

American military and industrial might? Look at what can be found.

For many years politicians and prominent figures around the world have spoken about a, 'New World Order', these include such individuals as George Herbert Walker Bush, Henry Kissinger, Tony Blair and Gordon Brown, to mention just a few. The words 'New World Order' are in themselves quite innocuous, but if one addresses the implications behind these words with regard to the world of politics and President Eisenhower's warning concerning the 'military industrial complex', they take on new and distinctly menacing implications.

It has been said many times that the actual motive behind the Gulf War was oil. Although there does seem to be some foundation to this point of view, it would appear that it was not the sole reason. In 2000, the Iraqi President Saddam Hussain was initiating the financial move from using the petro-dollar to using the Euro. Although at the time the Euro might not have been seen to be the most financially astute course for Iraq to take, it was nonetheless Iraq's choice to follow whatever direction it decided upon. This move would have had repercussions for both the United States of America and Britain, and so to put it simply, Iraq was attacked, instability reigned and the petro-dollar in Iraq was secured. The first of the seven countries was dealt a crippling blow. With Iraq now being unstable and in effect leaderless, a power vacuum had been created in the Middle-East. This Vacuum was to be filled by the terror group ISIS.

On October 20th 2011, Libya in North Africa was still undergoing a civil war, on the same day, Libyan leader Colonel Muammar Gaddafi was killed during the battle of Sirte. The death of Colonel Gaddafi marked the final death blow for Libya as a country to function under its own autonomous and independent government. It also marked the end of plans which Colonel Gaddafi had been attempting to put in place, to create an African currency. This currency unlike the American dollar and British pound would have tangible value; it would be backed by gold. Had Colonel Gaddafi been able to put an African currency backed by gold into place, then Africa would, instead of being the poor cousin, supported by the west and manipulated in all manner of ways, have been able to begin the process of self-sufficiency. There would without doubt have been disruptions and conflicts, but the African nations would over time have been able to counter the effects of drought, disease and political discontents, to name but a few points.

It would be fair to assume that neither Saddam Hussain nor Colonel Muammar Gaddafi were working with altruistic aims in mind. They were both powerful political leaders following their own material and ideological agendas. The political, social and financial paths of these two men crossed with an elite that were and are no less mercenary in their outlook and desire to attain their own goals by whatever means, also having no care or consideration for the consequences of their actions nor for the so called 'collateral damage' that always results. The 'collateral damage' often referred to by political, social and perhaps financial figures does not give any indication as to the true suffering of those poor wretches, the men, women and children who, through no fault of their own become casualties, often suffering horrific injuries, nor the many people who join the ever expanding list of fatalities world-wide.

Syria and Iran have in recent years both shifted away from the US dollar, the repercussions of which have been devastating for Syria and brought stiff measures against Iran. Syria has been in a state of civil war since 2011, a civil war that has been the cause of much suffering and many, many deaths. The argument that Bashar al-Assad as with Saddam Hussain and Colonel Gaddafi is a tyrant and should be removed from power does not justify the suffering that has been inflicted upon the people of Syria.

Iran has, since the removal of the Shah in 1979 been the target of Western propaganda and endless sanctions, and also been included by President George Bush in 2002 as part of the 'axis of evil'. With the West continuously undermining the geopolitical stability of the Middle-East, the whole region has become a political and religious powder keg, the igniting of which could easily have far reaching implications and effects world-wide.

Russia and China have always been major thorns in the side of those elite following the ideology of introducing a New World Order. For many years whilst these two countries followed a communist philosophy there was no real threat to the world elite and the concept of the N.W.O. Even when the cold war was at its height and the world was enveloped under the shadow of possible nuclear war, both the West and Russia knew only too well that in the event of a nuclear exchange, there could be no clear victor. But with the fall of communism in Russia and China taking more of a worldly outlook, those pursuing the notion of the N.W.O have become increasingly alarmed at their lack of clandestine influence in both Russia and China. Unlike the countries of the Middle-East, Africa and the South-American continent, Russia and China have enough social stability and cohesion so as to hinder, if not stop the elite of the N.W.O from gaining a foothold in their countries. One other factor that frustrates the elite are the military forces available to both countries. Unlike earlier mentioned nations, Russia and China both have considerable military assets at their disposal. Whereas earlier mentioned countries had neither the political and social cohesiveness nor the military strength and technology to block moves made against them that both Russia and China possess.

Russia has in recent times come under fire from Western governments, being accused of 'Hacking' computer systems world-wide including, affecting the United States presidential elections and power companies. Since then there have been a number of 'cyber attacks' world-wide. The source of these attacks has been stated as being Russia. Many people will be easily swayed to believe the 'Fake News' and propaganda poured forth, even though there is a distinct lack of proof. As the elite cannot cause direct harm to Russia for its stance in world affairs, it is using any means that may come to hand in an attempt to undermine yet another country's political and social administration. It has not been determined as to where these 'cyber attacks' originated from, but accusations continuously flow out while facts and proof are it would seem, no longer essential in the world. Whether Russia or any other country or its leadership is guilty of 'cyber attacks' or not is something that should be proven before both the media and political administrations make such damming accusations.

Countless allegations have been made against the leadership and governments of numerous countries over the past few years, many of which have been found to be unsubstantiated, 'Fake News'. Weapons of mass destruction in Iraq, gas attacks in Syria, supposedly authorised by Bashar al-Assad, 'cyber attacks' by Russia, the list goes on and on. There will always be political wrangling, but perhaps the world would be a better place if accusations were to be based on fact and proof. However, in the present age within which we live, fact and proof are often manufactured by the elite of the N.W.O to suit their needs. So even when proof is supplied it cannot always be trusted to be accurate as history has shown. If a lie is told and repeated often enough by the media and administration officials, it is often perceived by the population to be the truth.

Whistle-blowers

The world we live in today is not that different from the rest of human of history. Throughout our past the truth has often not been as important as the final outcome of a desired situation. Within the sphere of politics, political parties manufacture their individual manifestos with the aim of enticing elements of the population with the issues raised therein. They offer social improvements for the poor and the disenfranchised, persuading the differing social classes that their children will have better standards of education, medical care and housing. Yet once dominance in government has been achieved, the promises made, more often than not fall by the wayside. Politicians by their very nature avoid the truth, instead offering the appearance of sincerity while plying the public with platitudes for their lack of appropriate prosecution of their previously stated aims. Within the political realm it appears relatively easy to manipulate the truth, covering all manner of alleged misdeeds, but throughout the rest of society it is becoming more and more difficult to avoid the truth as increasing numbers of whistle-blowers come forward.

One of the most notable whistle-blowers of recent times is the American ex-CIA employee Edward Snowden. (Figure. 11) Edward Snowden 'leaked' information to the Guardian which the latter began releasing on June 13th 2013. The revelations were shocking, opening the eyes of the world to the way in which the security services function. The capabilities of the National Security Agency (NSA) and the Government Communications Headquarters (GCHQ), would stagger the minds of the average individual. The breadth and depth of the encroachment into the privacy of the individual in society is both morally and ethically questionable in a supposedly free and transparent society.

Information 'leaked' by Edward Snowden included items such as:

- Secret court orders allowing the NSA to take American citizens phone records,
- Revelations that Britain operated its own version of the NSA monitoring system of fiber optic cables around the world,
- The existence of something called Prism, a program that allowed for the processing of data supposedly requested from U.S tech giants such as Microsoft, Google, Facebook and others,
- The use of a system named Xkeyscore that is capable of searching through all information held on an individual. An analyst needs no authorization or clearance from a legal body such as a court to undertake this action.
- The implementation of efforts by the N.S.A to crack encryption on the internet. Therefore making internet security less effective, if not pointless.

It could be said that the N.S.A has been acting purely in the interests of the American population, keeping terrorists from the shores. If this were the case, then there would be no need to monitor internet traffic, texts and phone calls and also have access to the private information of American citizens. The escalation of information gathering went into 'overdrive' after the disaster of 9/11. The 'attack' on the World Trade Centre in 2001 gave the administration justification to expand their already extensive monitoring and data collection activities.
Edward Snowden while working for the security services realised that human rights, privacy and liberty were being eroded by the government itself under the pretext of national security. He therefore acted in what he believed to be the best interest of the general population and became a whistle-blower, informing the public that their own state was and is acting in a manner that is detrimental to the freedoms and rights that they hold in such high regard.

Fig.11

Edward Snowden, CIA whistle-blower
Wikipedia, The free Encyclopaedia.

At the present time it is believed that Edward Snowden is still residing in Russia where he has gained a certain amount of protection from those who desire his extradition. The desire of the American administration to prosecute this man for his actions seems unjustified when addressing the dubious ploys undertaken by them to undermine foreign governments and affect regime change.

Chelsea (formally Bradley) Manning was a 25 year old US private, who whilst in US army intelligence downloaded more than 700,000 classified files from United States military servers. He then forwarded the documents to WikiLeaks.
Again, an individual working on his/her own with the aim of informing the world of unlawful activity. It could be said that the releasing of this information might cause loss of American lives, yet the publishing of this material has already proven wrong doing and that a loss of lives had already taken place, the deaths of foreign nationals in their own countries.

On the 5th April 2010 WikiLeaks made open to the public a US military video showing the unselective killing and wounding of a number of people in the Iraqi suburb of New Baghdad, in 2007. The video was taken by a camera fixed to the gunsight of a United States Apache helicopter and was immediately designated as classified by the U.S military. Two Reuter's news staff who were involved in the attack by the Apache helicopter also died along with the Iraqi civilians.

The many documents that have been released by WikiLeaks are too numerous to mention here, documents that have been provided by whistleblowers; not for personal gain or fame, nor to purposely damage the military or government, but because these whistleblowers have seen or become aware of inappropriate, erroneous and often unlawful material of which the general populations should be made aware. In the above example, the individuals might well have been incorrectly identified and therefore have been perceived as posing a serious threat, but that is not the point. Why would the video have been classified if it were simply a case of either self-defense or acting in the defense of others?

Chelsea (Bradley) Manning was convicted by court-martial in July of 2013 and sentenced to 35 years imprisonment. After almost seven years' incarceration, President Barak Obama commuted the sentence and Chelsea Manning walked back into society. It is interesting to note that Chelsea Manning revealed significant information relating to abuse and cover-up, information that should have been released immediately by the authorities, yet, rather than being acknowledged for doing the right thing, had her own human rights infringed upon by being imprisoned.

The commutation of Chelsea Manning's sentence gained this response from Senator John McCain, chairman of the Senate armed services committee, stating that this,

When Senator McCain speaks of 'the proper channels', he is neglecting to address the evidence that material is all too often classified immediately. This leaves the individual the unenviable task of becoming a whistle-blower and with no other option than to act on their own initiative, keeping their principles, as do the majority of Americans, intact and untainted by the corruptive influences that would prefer that the truth should not surface.

In 1945 the National Security Agency (NSA) initiated an undertaking named Project shamrock. This project was to gather all telegrams and similar communications, (this included correspondence of U.S citizens) both entering and exiting the Unites States.   It should be noted that this project was undertaken allegedly without court authorization or warrants being issued.   Project shamrock was allegedly related to the setup of Project Minaret which ran from the 1960's until the early 1970's. Project Minaret was also administered under the control of the N.S.A, its objective was to monitor the communications of selected American citizens who voiced anti-Vietnam sentiments. These selected Americans included such individuals as Martin Luther King Jr, a leading figure in the American civil rights movement and Mohammad Ali the world champion boxer, also two notable members of Congress, Senator Frank Church (Democrat-Idaho) and Senator Howard Baker (Republican–Tennessee).

It would seem that Senator McCain's 'proper channels' might well be untrustworthy as has been indicated above, in that they are scrutinizing, censoring and abusing their own citizenry. If influential elements within one's own government are considered to be operating under their own agenda, then what other course would one have but to deliver material to an organisation that is capable of ensuring that it gets into the public arena. When the actions, acts and laws infringe upon the very populous whose lives they are purportedly said to protect, whether they be national or international, then 'whistle-blowers' should be praised for their selfless acts and not vilified and imprisoned.

The world is indeed in a sad state when people refuse to acknowledge what is happening around them and so bury their heads deeper into the propaganda filled sand.

Growth of a New World Order

The label of 'conspiracy theorist' has been mockingly placed upon the shoulders of many who have questioned the true purpose and motives of such organisations as the Bilderberg group, the Trilateral commission and the Council on Foreign Relations. These private and self-professed non-partisan bodies have gained a reputation world-wide for being very influential within political, industrial and financial fields. Their activities can have an impact across many borders.

The Bilderberg Group

As larger numbers of people world-wide are becoming aware of the Bilderberg group, more questions are being asked as to its actual purpose, what its true function is in the world. As some individuals will already be aware, the Bilderberg group came into existence in 1954 and is said to have been established by Prince Bernhard of Lippe-Biesterfeld. The location of the first meeting was the Hotel De Bilderberg in Oosterbeek, Netherlands, from the 29th to the 31st of May of the same year. The aim was stated as being 'to promote communication between North America and Europe'. Since that time there have been regular yearly meetings and it should be emphasised that participation is by invite only. These invited guests include prominent figures from the spheres of politics, industry and finance to mention but a few.

The official Bilderberg website states that,

"The meeting is a forum for informal discussions about megatrends and major issues facing the world." It goes on to say, *"...the participants are not bound by the conventions of their office or by pre-agreed positions."*

http://bilderbergmeetings.org/index.html

The words above give the impression that a lot of extremely influential people gather together over tea and biscuits, just having a bit of a chat about what is happening in the world. The Bilderberg group is depicted as having an almost altruistic purpose, with general concern for the world as a whole and the population therein being its primary concern. To assume the previous sentence to be an accurate estimation of the true nature and aims of all of those who attend these meetings would be naïve to say the least. With so many influential and powerful individuals gathering together in this fashion, it would be ludicrous to suggest that policies, within the frameworks of politics, finances and industry, to mention but a few, could not be and are not affected. Although policy is established by governmental authorities, this does not mean that it cannot be and is not surreptitiously influenced by external sources, and to suggest otherwise would be to show childlike qualities that would not be out of place in a kindergarten.

Bilderbergers, those who attend the Bilderberg meetings are charged with paying for their own travel and accommodation, although security for the meetings is ostensibly sourced and funded by the Bilderberg group itself. The Bilderberg group does not pay for all of the required facilities as with the case of the meeting at the Grove Hotel near Watford in England, where the local police forces were required to supply additional services and support. The expenditure for these police forces comes directly from their own limited budgets. In other words the taxpayers of the host country, through the police forces, are actually paying towards the costs of the Bilderberg meetings.

The high degree of narcissism of those who attend such meetings is mirrored by the high levels of security that they consider themselves to need, this is especially noteworthy as they are supposedly not undertaking official business. As the participants are not constrained by the principles and confines that their office or position would normally necessitate, this begs the question as to where they loyalties lay? Is their allegiance with the nation that they represent politically, financially or industrially? Or are they loyal to the principles and dogmas of the

Bilderberg group and its associates? The meetings follow what is known as the 'Chatham House rule'.

The 'Chatham House' rule comes from Chatham House, the Royal Institute of International Affairs in London, founded in 1920. The 'rule' came into existence in 1927 and was refined in 1992 and 2002.

https://www.chathamhouse.org/

The Chatham House Rule is as follows:

"When a meeting, or part thereof, is held under the Chatham House Rule, participants are free to use the information received, but neither the identity nor the affiliation of the speaker(s), nor that of any other participant, may be revealed."

https://www.chathamhouse.org/

As is stated above, *"...participants are free to use the information received..."* With no record of exactly what information is divulged by participants within the meeting, (unless that information has been purposely released by members) and no monitoring body, the question of national security arises. Participants can divulge information as they see fit, information that may be used by other participants to whatever ends, yet neither the information nor the identity of the individual disclosing information may be revealed. As these meetings are not sanctioned by governmental bodies and there is no oversight body assigned, it is understandable as to why the populations of countries have serious objections concerning the Bilderberg group.

Edward Snowden has been vilified for whistleblowing, revealing information that has made the world aware of a number of certain organisations' immoral and unethical practices, yet those powerful and influential men and women who attend the Bilderberg meeting appear not to be held to the same rules that apply within their professional offices, this should therefore raise serious questions as to the legality of certain individuals attending these meetings, especially under the Chatham house rule.

With the lack of candour surrounding the Bilderberg group, one cannot help but recall a quote by the British Conservative Member of Parliament for Gloucester, Richard Graham,

> *"...if you have nothing to hide, you have nothing to fear."*

Michael Deacon, Telegraph. 04 Nov 2015.

The words were spoken in defence of a government surveillance bill proposed by the then Home Secretary, Theresa May. The actual origin of the quote is unknown, although it is often attributed to the world war two German Minister of Propaganda, Joseph Goebbels. So, if the British population must be monitored to an even higher degree, presumably for their own safety, then one must surely enquire as to why the Bilderberg group should likewise not be monitored and their meetings brought out into the open for public scrutiny. After all, as the British government said, "If you have nothing to hide, you have nothing to fear."

The Trilateral commission

The Trilateral Commission was founded by private citizens in July of 1973 under the guidance of David Rockefeller, who was at the time chairman of the Council on Foreign Relations. The stated aim of this commission was to foster relations between Japan, Europe and the United States. Over time the Trilateral Commission has grown considerably, now having many international and influential figures amongst its membership, also there are three separate groups both within and under the umbrella and influence of the main body of the Trilateral Commission. These three separate groups convene for yearly meetings, as does the main body of the Trilateral Commission. Unlike the Bilderberg group, the Trilateral Commission does permit the general public to peruse the various reports from meetings and tasks undertaken. By making these reports available to society, the Trilateral Commission has been endeavouring to show an openness that will gain the trust of the population, offering reassurances that all is 'above board', and that the aims and objectives of the Trilateral Commission are beyond reproach.

The official Trilateral Commission website states,

"To help preserve the commission's unofficial character, members who take up positions in their national administration give up Trilateral Commission membership."

http://trilateral.org/

This apparent ethical stance will undoubtedly offer reassurance to the populace, in that theoretically no member, whist being a representative of their national administration in one capacity or another, can influence or be influenced by the Trilateral Commission, or by its membership. The idea of an administrational body not being subject to influence from the Trilateral Commission can have no basis in reality. Members can go from being part of the Trilateral Commission, to being part of an administration and then back to the Trilateral Commission once again. It would be preposterous to suggest that they would operate in a fashion that would exclude the ideas and beliefs of the Commission. As membership of the Commission is by invite only and the aim is to foster relations, then it is reasonable to assume that the beliefs and socio-economic philosophies of the members must coincide. Principle beliefs of human beings become an intrinsic part of their character, therefore the same beliefs and values would logically transfer with an individual from one position to another, and so from the Trilateral Commission to a particular administrational position.

Council on Foreign Relations

The body of the Council on Foreign Relations is made up solely of United States Citizens and was founded in 1921. As with the Bilderberg group and the Trilateral commission, it is stated as being a non-partisan organisation, a 'think tank' with the aim of gaining a better understanding of the,

"...world and the foreign policy choices facing the United States and other countries".

https://www.cfr.org/who-we-are/mission-statement

Again, as with the previously mentioned organisations, its membership for the most part is assembled from the higher echelons of American society, bankers, lawyers, politicians, etc., individuals who are or will become influential in world matters. On the website of the Council on Foreign Relations it states that the CFR,

"...takes no institutional positions on matters of policy and has no affiliation with the U.S. government".

https://www.cfr.org/who-we-are/faqs

The above quote could be seen as not being decidedly plausible and also rather farfetched in its claim, if not actually misleading. The statement would not be out of place in some imaginary world that might be associated with such works as Aldous Huxley's, Brave New World, or Thomas Moore's, Utopia.

The membership of the Council on Foreign Relations is indeed impressive, individuals include; Madeleine Albright, (former) Secretary of State, David Rockefeller, John Abizaid, (former) Commander-in-Chief, United States Central Command, Kenneth M. Duberstein, (former) White House Chief of Staff and Henry Kissinger, (former) U.S. Secretary of State, to mention but a few. As much of the membership have been associated with administrational policy or have been part of the administration at one time or another, and given that beliefs and values become an intrinsic part of an individual's character, it would seem absurd to state that the Council on Foreign Relations and its membership have no affiliation with the U.S Government. The same rationale is applicable to the lack of institutional opinion when it comes to issues of policy. As with the Trilateral Commission and the Bilderberg Group, the Council on Foreign Relations portrays itself with an almost altruistic motive for its existence. For these organisations to be defined as non-partisan given the associations between them and the worlds of politics, finance and industry, could be expressed as, 'stretching the bounds of accuracy', to say the very least.

The membership of the previously mentioned organisations do, due to their social, financial and political influences wield incredible power internationally. Their influence transcends national borders, financial institutions and the military. Decisions are made behind closed doors that have far-reaching effects for the populations of countries worldwide. Utilising information that has been gathered, presumably by such organisations as the NSA under the guise of national security, they affect the lives of millions if not billions of people, manipulating and changing social and economic norms and values. The final goal of such organisations is globalisation. According to the Cambridge dictionary globalisation is defined as,

"...the increase of trade around the world, especially by large companies producing and trading goods in many different countries." The definition continues as, "...a situation where available goods and services, or social and cultural influences, gradually become similar in all parts of the world".

http://dictionary.cambridge.org/dictionary/english/globalization

Initially bringing the people of this world together under common aims, values and beliefs might seem a desirable and laudable objective, and indeed would and does have merit, but it is the means by which this goal is achieved that comes into question. The elite of this world have gained even greater wealth, power and influence, at the expense of the ordinary person. People have suffered and died across the world whilst the military-industrial complex has firmly tightened its grasp about the throats of unwitting populations; prices have risen, foods have been genetically altered, quality medical care is available for those few who can afford it, and the distance between the elite and the rest of society has grown into a chasm and is still expanding at an exponential rate. The underlying attitude that emanates from the global elite is one of arrogant superiority. The misuse of authority and distain shown for the general population has allowed the birth of a new social class, that of the Precariat.

The term precariat is an amalgam of the words *precious* and *proletariat.* According to Wikipedia, the precariat refers to,

> *"...a social class formed by people suffering from precarity, which is a condition of existence without predictability or security, affecting material or psychological welfare".*

https://en.wikipedia.org/wiki/Precariat

In his 2011 book, The Precariat: A Dangerous New Class, Professor Guy Standing gets the point clearly across that the precariat is rapidly growing, and that,

> *"...the greater the size, the more the dysfunctional aspects will grow ominous".*

The Precariat: A Dangerous New Class

Globalisation is not necessarily the harmless and innocent endeavour that has been portrayed by the elite. It has caused and is causing a breakdown in social values and pushing the vast majority of the population into financial debt. This debt is something that cannot be not easily avoided. With the introduction of fiat money and the dissolving of the gold standard, the debt of nations has grown to the point where it cannot be easily, if ever discharged. Laws are manipulated and financial advantages granted to corporations at the expense of the population.

As more and more people feel the lack of purpose in their lives being thrust upon them and the inescapable descent into social and financial poverty, the more dysfunctional their society becomes. With little or no security and predictability in their lives and the dysfunctionality of society increasing, the precariat is rapidly growing as the lives of ever more people spiral down out of their control. Inevitably, as the precariat expands, social unrest keeps equal pace with this steadily growing behemoth. The distain shown for those of the precariat by the global elite does and will increase levels of resentment and voices raised in anger, and in this way the precariat can easily become a dangerous threat to those of the elite. There is little in the way of incentives for those of the precariat to adhere to the politics and policies of the present administrations, and would be more than likely, as history has shown many times before, to adhere to more extreme left and right wing politics.

The precariat is not an uneducated mass, it is socially, politically and financially cognisant of the world around it and also the injustices, both moral and ethical that have taken place, forcing individuals into the social class within which they now find themselves. Due to a general dissatisfaction of the existing politically established parties, and amid a growing resentment of the elite, a new and extreme political movement could easily arise, having its roots firmly based in the precariat, the disenfranchised and the under-classes. The people have little confidence and belief in the ability of governments to improve society, instead they see an elite gaining power, influence and wealth, improving their own situations at the expense of the average person.

As professor Standing points out,

> *"In the age of the precariat, loyalty and trust are contingent and fragile".*

The Precariat: A Dangerous New Class

These very accurate words should raise concern. As the general public are manipulated by governments, banking organisations and the business world, levels of trust have plummeted. The belief of the elite that the populace will ravenously digest the propaganda poured forth is gravely misguided. With greater numbers of people world-wide 'awakening' from their almost reverie like state of belief in the elite, society has begun to lose its cohesion. It is not only the precariat that have begun to resist the efforts of the powerful elite to take nations into a one world government. Opposition has been slowly but surely gaining momentum across the world throughout the spectrum of differing social classes, dissention is being voiced with greater numbers of people joining demonstrations in the streets of their countries. This dissent could be thought to be just a natural consequence of change, the resistance to progress, and the notion that people often cannot see what is best for them and so must be coerced by whatever means into the future. This reasoning could be said to have a certain plausibility except for the fact that the global elite are increasing their wealth, power and influence at the expense and dreadful suffering of an enormous part of the world's population.

The very idea of a global elite attempting to establish a one world government is often ridiculed by authoritative figures, placing any such suggestion firmly into the realms of 'conspiracy theory' and 'fake news'. All too often people see their own social and financial situation as being secure, protected from outside influences, ignoring the fact that their position in life can change at any moment and for the most obscure of reasons. In an attempt to ensure security in their lives people become 'Yes' men or women, willing to sacrifice others in the false hope of keeping control of their own lives, committing actions at the behest of others that they know to be morally and or ethically wrong. This is one of the foundations upon which the global elite have built their control and power.

The population condition

If the notion of an elite global cabal working to gain control of the lives of individuals seems like an exaggerated fantasy, then perhaps the words of Professor Carroll Quigley, historian and theorist, might aid people in awakening from their artificially induced reverie. A reverie not self-created, but brought about by the manipulations of the very elite that people innocently and mistakenly believe to be improving the quality of their lives.
Professor Carroll Quigley of Georgetown University, in his 1966 book: Tragedy and Hope, 'A History of the World in Our Time', stated that financial powers have the aim,

"...to create a world system of financial control in private hands able to dominate the political system of each country and the economy of the world as a whole."

Professor Carroll Quigley, Tragedy and Hope. 1966.

Within a remarkably short period of time and with the consent of populations (although unwittingly), the above aim has to all intents and purposes been achieved.   The dissolution of the gold standard and the creation of 'fiat' money have greatly assisted the elite in allowing them to gain control of financial systems worldwide. Through the production of 'fiat' money and control of the world's financial markets, commodities that are held to be essential in the modern world are regulated by the elite, foodstuffs, medical drugs, fuel (gas, electricity, petrol), and many other products are controlled. This is not done for the reasons that are all too often given, such as saving the environment, reducing the effects of climate change, or 'saving the planet', but for the benefit of the few, by which means they gain greater influence both financially and politically. This leaves the vast majority of the world's population suffering in numerous ways, too many to mention here. Billions of people struggle each day to feed themselves and their families due to an elite that is in effect 'playing God', by attempting to create a one world government without the consent of the world's population.

People do have a massive impact upon nature, but the likely hood that people are solely responsible for the level of climate change claimed, is preposterous. Populations are coerced into believing that they are either directly or indirectly responsible for the damage being done to the environment, yet it is those who effect the deregulation of laws that permit companies to negatively affect and damage the environment who are culpable. In response to the exaggerated claims regarding climate change, governments and non-partisan organisations have created artificial strategies for environmental sustainability.

"Movement towards sustainability has to be reconciled with drives towards deregulation and economic growth"

Sustainable Development: Agenda 21 and Earth Summit II
Research Paper 96/87, 16 August 1996

Sustainability of the natural environment cannot be reconciled with economic growth in the present age, particularly by removing regulations put in place to preserve nature, the countryside and sea and their fauna and flora. To give an example of the incompatibility of environmental sustainability and economic growth, one might address the population of whales in the world's oceans. With the population of whales in the world already dwindling, their number cannot be sustained or increased by removing regulations that ensure their survival, bearing in mind that whales are killed for profit, in other words economic reasons.

Perhaps it should be pointed out that enormous climate changes are something that have apparently been taking place upon the earth since it was initially formed. The earth does not need us to save 'it', this planet will be here long after the human race has become extinct, through either self-annihilation or through some evolutionary process. Climate change is to a large degree being used as a means of frightening and manipulating populations into submissiveness, quietly acquiescing to the orders and requirements of the global elite.

The world is within an age where people discard all manner of items rather than getting them repaired, a 'throw away mentality or society'. Individuals now always desire something of a newer design or seemingly better quality. This is not surprising as consumerism has 'turned the heads' of so many in society into believing that it is part of the natural order of things.

Governments and numerous corporations portray consumerism as essential for the economic growth of a country, and as such also for the benefit of the population as a whole. Yet this is not the case. It is not the population who gain from the misguided levels of consumerism, the root of which originates from the Latin 'Consumo', meaning, 'To waste', but the very corporations and manufacturers themselves and more often than not, the members of a particular government or those closely associated with both. If sustainability were the true desire of governments and supposedly non-partisan organisations, then surely these organisations would endeavour to ensure that the manufacturing industries produced goods that can easily and cheaply be repaired, rather than being constantly replaced. Focus would be directed away from the mass production items that create immense recycling problems, instead addressing repairs and improvements to the items already possessed without dramatically increasing costs. One should have no doubt the public would be given innumerable fictitious reasons as to why repairs and improvements that are cost effective would be neither practicable nor possible. If the population can be manipulated as has been the case to become more materialistic, believing that they need all manner of possessions for their lives to be fulfilled, then these people can easily over time be shown that this just is not the case. People do not need such an immense quantity of material items as they have been led to believe by the manufacturing industries. Society is filled with people desperately attempting to improve their lives and social status and constantly struggling financially, in debt to the financial sectors that fund and or run the very manufactories that produce the items that are neither of any particular intrinsic value nor improve quality of life or social status.

One of the simplest of ways for any social elite to gain the confidence of the people and therefore control of power in society is to ensure that the attention of the population has been taken in at least one other direction. With the focus of the common people drawn in different directions, it is unlikely that they will notice that their 'rights' whether in common law or under admiralty law have been eroded. In fact the majority will accept any changes with little or no opposition, concentrating instead on the falsely created distractions. Through a general and somewhat naïvely accepted belief, the vast proportion of the population see their 'lords and masters' working only for either the benefit of the population or the country, or both. Those few who do realise and can see what has been or is occurring often raise their frustrations as though voices in the wilderness, while the common people slumber in their trusting innocence and obedience.

An array of social distractions often used by elite elements include such things as; consumerism and climate change as mentioned earlier. Other distractions can and do include such awful actions as terrorism and war. Terrorism is a very real threat in the present age, but perhaps if one were to address the origins of modern terrorism, its creators and those who fund such evil deeds, then and only then would one see with clarity that all is not as it seems. The military actions and wars undertaken by western nations, sending their young men and women to fight and die in an effort to stop the very terrorists that were and are created and funded by western governments and or their allies, are but another side of the same coin. As has been said so frequently by those who recognise the dangers in modern society, the elite utilise a very simple and practiced design for social control, that of; Problem, Reaction, Solution. To mould the population within whatever parameters the elite desire, a problem must be in existence that can be reacted to and then a solution found and applied. Although the initial 'Problem' will generally be fictitious in its origin, it will have its basis in reality such as terrorism or climate change. The problem soon gains a solid foothold in the minds and hearts of the masses through instillation of a fear mentality, thus the 'Reaction' via manipulation of the truth. The reaction of fear that permeates through the population is exploited by the elite, who are then able to offer the distressed masses a 'Solution'. The 'Solution' invariably includes such measures as greatly increased surveillance of the population itself, the erosion of self-expression through political correctness, the limiting of freedom of speech and increased levels of redundant bureaucracy.

People willingly accept the changes in their lives through the process of cognitive dissonance. When a moral or ethical conflict arises within society, differing beliefs or values, the population are told by the elite that it is imperative that a balance be found. The elite present options, leading heavily in one direction, and the masses, immaterial of their personal moral and ethical values follow blindly, as sheep to slaughter, believing all the while that they still have the ability to make their own decisions. Finally, personal rights of the individual are consigned to the history books in favour of Orwellian laws and an increase in national security. The population unwittingly hand their lives and the lives of their loved ones over to an elite who have strived for and almost achieved a dystopian state.

The Final Cut

The magnitude of transformations being undertaken by the global elite through-out all aspects of society; industrially, financially, politically, militarily and socially, is staggering. Millions of individuals are needlessly suffering due to the efforts of a few powerful people attempting to lay the foundations for a new world order. While the vast majority of the population are unaware of the true ramifications of the creation of a 'New World Order' under the direct control of a single governing body, their silence is taken as approval. People are being deceived via misleading information, direct manipulation or simply not being made aware of facts, so they do not protest. This lack of protestation, in other words their silence is taken as consent,

> *"Qui tacet consentire videtur "*, this literally means, *"Who is silent is seen to consent."*

The population are therefore in agreement with the changes across all aspects of society, this leaves the people as powerless, unable to contest the validity and true legal status of any legislation that will or may be brought into being on any future occasion.

Social morals and ethics are rapidly being worn away by the steady manipulations of a small yet elite element within society whose aim is purely and simply the desire for power and wealth, even though it be at the expense of the lives of millions. Any individual that is perceived as a possible risk to the undertakings of the elite are designated socially and politically as undesirable or dissident. There are many in society who will refuse to see what is right in front of them, preferring instead to live with the knowledge that they are not presently being affected in any seriously manner.

To those individuals, the words of Pastor Martin Niemoller, a German anti-Nazi theologian and Lutheran pastor should perhaps be noted,

"First they came for the Socialists, and I did not speak out—
Because I was not a Socialist.

Then they came for the Trade Unionists, and I did not speak
out—
Because I was not a Trade Unionist.

Then they came for the Jews, and I did not speak out—
Because I was not a Jew.

Then they came for me—and there was no one left to speak for
me."

Pastor Martin Niemolle, Holocaust Encyclopedia.

It should be noted that one can bury one's head in the sand but the rest of the body is still visible, so living with the misguided belief that if one follows the rules, albeit rule supposedly through jurisprudence, one is not immune to the extreme effects that eventually rear their head.

The ludicrous degree to which the population accept the duplicity of certain legislation is visible in the United Kingdom with the introduction of what is known as the 'bail-in'. If banks or other financial institutions enter extreme financial difficulties, then rather than the government bailing out the institution financially, the onus and expense will be borne by the depositors, much to their detriment. What this means is that the man and woman in the street will have funds removed from their accounts to ensure the stability of the institution. The very bankers who have created much of the discord in the world and who are millionaires or billionaires, now have the general population to fall back on and keep them in the life style to which they have become accustomed. So the population who already pay tax on their accounts, also pay interest and other banking charges, will in fact be paying for their own servitude. This is just another example of the elite exploiting opportunistic events whereby they have managed to take advantage of a situation with considerable success, duping the public while portraying their actions as being for the benefit of the population at large.

The ideas mentioned within this work would not sound out of place in a Dan Brown novel. But sadly they do not originate from a work of fiction, but in the real world, the world that we all reside within. With all of the convolutions and intrigue in the modern world, and the desire of people for continuity within their lives, it is perhaps understandable that many would refute claims of a one world government and a new world order. But when all other options have been exhausted, and proof is laid out for all to clearly see, perhaps then people will pay attention and stand up to stop the expansion of something that is without doubt a significant threat to the world's population as a whole. As Arthur Conan Doyle's character Sherlock Holmes stated,

"...when you have eliminated all which is impossible, then whatever remains, however improbable, must be the truth."

Arthur Conan Doyle, The Blanched Soldier, 1926.

If people could only learn that there is far more than this world we live upon, more than just this galaxy and universe that we live within, that we all are so much more than we are either told or believe, then perhaps, just perhaps we might learn to see...

Bibliography

The Precariat: A Dangerous New Class. Professor Guy Standing, Bloomsbury. (2011). Pp. 58.

Shifting Mandates: The Federal Reserve's First Centennial, Carmen M. Reinhart and Kenneth S. Rogoff. (2013).

The United States Government Manual, (1991/92)

Office of the Federal Register National Archives and Records Administration.

Register of Corporations, Directors and Executives, Standard and Poor. (1991).

Annual Report, The Council On Foreign Relations, Pratt House, New York City, (*1991/92*).

The Blanched Soldier. Arthur Conan Doyle. (1926). Pp. 8.

Tragedy and Hope: A History of the World in Our Time. Professor Carroll Quigley, Macmillan Company, NEW YORK. (1966) Pp. 324.

Winning Modern Wars: Iraq, Terrorism, and the American Empire, Gen. Wesley Clark, Public Affairs, N.Y, (2003).

Newspapers

"Theresa May, the new spy laws... and a warning for the public, The Telegraph, Michael Deacon", (04 Nov 2015).

"British taxpayers to pay 'millions' towards secretive Bilderberg meeting security", The Telegraph, Rowena Mason, 30 May 2013.

"Oswald 'had no time to fire all Kennedy bullets'", The Telegraph, Tim Shipman. (01 Jul 2007)

"Revealed: the men with stolen identities", The Telegraph, David Harrison. (23 Sep 2001).

"Bradley Manning trial: what we know from the leaked WikiLeaks documents", The Guardian, Peter Walker. (30 July 2013).

"Chelsea Manning's prison sentence commuted by Barak Obama", Pilkington, Smith and Gambino, The Guardian. (18th January, 2017).

****

World Wide Web

http://www.presidency.ucsb.edu/

https://www.brainyquote.com/quotes/authors/j/james_madison.html

http://www.bilderbergmeetings.org/

https://www.cfr.org/

https://www.cfr.org/content/about/*annual_report*/ar_2015/AR2015

https://www.chathamhouse.org/

http://dictionary.cambridge.org/dictionary/english/*globalization*

30-Year Anniversary: Tonkin Gulf Lie Launched Vietnam War, Cohen and Solomon - *http://fair.org/media-beat-column/30-year-anniversary-tonkin-gulf-lie-launched-vietnam-war/*

Holocaust Encyclopedia - https://www.ushmm.org/wlc/en/article.php?ModuleId=10007392

http://mashable.com/2014/06/05/edward-snowden-revelations/

National archives - *www.archives.gov/research/military/vietnam-war/casualty-statistics.html*

"Operation Northwoods" -
http://nsarchive.gwu.edu/news/20010430/northwoods.pdf

https://collateralmurder.wikileaks.org/

*http://researchbriefings.files.parliament.uk/documents/SN02599/SN0
2599*

*https://www.schneier.com/blog/archives/2005/12/project_shamroc.h
tml*

*http://www.telegraph.co.uk/news/uknews/7066383/David-Kelly-
death-evidence-to-be-kept-secret-for-70-years*

http://www.telegraph.co.uk/news/politics/theresa-may/11975789/

http://trilateral.org/

*http://truepublica.org.uk/united-kingdom/grand-theft-auto-uk-eu-
bank-depositor-bail-regime-implemented/*

http://www.sweetliberty.org/

https://en.wikipedia.org/wiki/*Precariat*

"Bilderberg Conference: Watford Mayor's concern over policing costs"-
http://www.bbc.co.uk/news/uk-england-beds-bucks-herts-22793804

"Bobby Hargis" -
http://mcadams.posc.mu.edu/hargis.htm

"Grand Theft Auto – UK and EU Bank Depositor Bail-In Regime
Implemented" -
http://truepublica.org.uk/united-kingdom/grand-theft-auto-uk-eu-
bank-depositor-bail-regime-implemented/

"Greenpeace" -
http://www.greenpeace.org/international/en/press/releases/2016/Fu
kushima-nuclear-disaster-will-impact-forests-rivers-and-estuaries-for-
hundreds-of-years-warns-Greenpeace-report-/

Bank Recovery and Resolution Directive (BRRD) implementation, (3rd November 2016) -
https://www.gov.uk/government/consultations/consultation-on-the-implementation-of-the-bank-recovery-and-resolution-directive-brrd/bank-recovery-and-resolution-directive-brrd-implementation

"CHART: Inflation Since 1775 And How It Took Off In 1933", Business Insider, Sam Ro, (Jan. 6, 2013) -
http://www.businessinsider.com/chart-inflation-since-1775-2013-1?IR=T

"At Least 7 of the 9/11 Hijackers are Still Alive", What really happened-
http://www.whatreallyhappened.com/WRHARTICLES/hijackers.html

https://en.wikipedia.org/wiki/Gulf_of_Tonkin_incident

"The Truth About Tonkin", U.S Navel Institute, Volume 22, Number 1. (February 2008) -
https://www.usni.org/magazines/navalhistory/2008-02/truth-about-tonkin

"Road blocks, police helicopters and blacked-out windows:" Mail Online, Simon Tomlinson, (6th June 2013) -
http://www.dailymail.co.uk/news/article-2336847/Bilderberg-2013-Who-billionaires-politicians-arriving-secretive-conference-Watford-hotel.html.

"A Brief History of the NSA: From 1917 to 2014", Michael X. Heiligenstein, (April 17, 2014) -
http://www.saturdayeveningpost.com/2014/04/17/culture/politics/a-brief-history-of-the-nsa.html

Integrating Neuroscience, Centre of Biomedical Research -
https://www.unr.edu/neuroscience/center/core-facilities/neuroimaging-core/fmri
"The Kelly Affair: Anatomy of a conspiracy theory", The Independent Online, Paul Vallely. (Friday 20 August 2010) –
http://www.independent.co.uk/news/uk/home-news/the-kelly-affair-anatomy-of-a-conspiracy-theory-2058065.html

"New documents reveal parameters of NSA's secret surveillance programs", The Washington Post, Nakashima, Gellman, Miller, (June 20th 2013) -
https://www.washingtonpost.com/world/national-security/new-documents-reveal-parameters-of-nsas-secret-surveillance-programs/

"The "War on Terror" is a Big Lie, ISIS is "Made in America"", Global Research, Centre for Research on Globalization, (March 10, 2015) -
http://www.globalresearch.ca/the-war-on-terror-is-a-big-lie-conference/5435592

"Professors & Politicians Gather To Warn Us About The New World Order (NWO)", Collective Evolution, Arjun Walia. (October 27th 2015) -
http://www.collective-evolution.com/2015/10/27/professors-politicians-gather-to-warn-us-about-the-new-world-order

"David Kelly death evidence 'to be kept secret for 70 years'", The Telegraph, (24 Jan 2010) -
http://www.telegraph.co.uk/news/uknews/7066383/David-Kelly-death-evidence-to-be-kept-secret-for-70-years.html

"Hutton inquiry closed David Kelly medical reports for 70 years", The Guardian, Afua Hirsch. (Monday 25 January 2010) -
https://www.theguardian.com/politics/2010/jan/25/david-kelly-suicide-hutton-inquiry

Public Inquiries: non-statutory commissions of inquiry: Number 02599. (30 November 2016) -
http://researchbriefings.files.parliament.uk/documents/SN02599/SN02599.pdf

"Another Snowden Leak: NSA Program Taps Everything You Do Online", MashableUk, Amanda Wills. (July 31 2013) –
http://mashable.com/2013/07/31/nsa-xkeyscore/#IaThbC20nsqh

"Declassified NSA files show agency spied on Mohammad Ali and MLK", The Guardian, Ed Pilkington. (26th September 2013) -
https://www.theguardian.com/world/2013/sep/26/nsa-surveillance-anti-vietnam-muhammad-ali-mlk

"Sustainable Development: Agenda 21 and Earth Summit II, Research Paper 96/87", Patsy Hughes, Science and Environment Section House of Commons Library. (16 August 1996) - http://researchbriefings.files.parliament.uk/documents/RP96-87/RP96-87.pdf

"Three Mile Island" – http://www.world-nuclear.org/information-library/safety-and-security/safety-of-plants/three-mile-island-accident.aspx

"Tony Blair showed 'little appetite' to ensure Iraq War was legal, Chilcot report says", Independent, Andy McSmith, (6 July 2016) – *http://www.independent.co.uk/news/uk/politics/chilcot-report-lord-goldsmith-legal-advice-iraq-war-tony-blair-verdict-latest-news-a7122756.html*

Statement by Sir John Chilcot: The Iraq Inquiry. (6 July 2016) - *http://www.iraqinquiry.org.uk/media/247010/2016-09-06-sir-john-chilcots-public-statement.pdf*

****

Images:

MRI – https://www.unr.edu/neuroscience/center/core-facilities/neuroimaging-core/fmri

President J. F. Kennedy, John F. Kennedy Presidential Library and Museum.

CHART: Inflation Since 1775 And How It Took Off In 1933, Business Insider, Sam Ro, (Jan. 6, 2013). *http://www.businessinsider.com/chart-inflation-since-1775-2013-1?IR=T*

Pont de Alma tunnel -

http://knkx.org/post/scotland-yard-assessing-new-information-diana-death

USS Rhode Island -
http://navylive.dodlive.mil/2013/07/19/ssbn-force-level-requirements-its-simply-a-matter-of-geography/
G.C.H.Q – Aerial view of Doughnut,
https://www.gchq.gov.uk/news

Edward Snowden -
https://en.wikipedia.org/wiki/Edward_Snowden

Gulf of Tonkin -
https://en.wikipedia.org/wiki/Gulf_of_Tonki

USS Maddox - Huffpost, The worldpost,
http://www.huffingtonpost.com/adst/august-2nd-the-gulf-of-to_b_11303432.html.

****

9/11 south tower collapse video -
https://www.youtube.com/watch?v=x91XXip8a5M

****